KV-373-717

Kathie Webber's Book of Autumn Cooking

SPHERE BOOKS LIMITED
30/32 Gray's Inn Road, London, WC1X 8JL

First published in Great Britain in 1978 by
Elm Tree Books/Hamish Hamilton Ltd
90 Great Russell Street
London WC1B 3PT
and
Sphere Books Ltd
30/32 Gray's Inn Road
London WC1X 8JL

Jacket photograph by Mike Leale
Illustrations by Su Turner

TRADE
MARK

Printed in Great Britain by Cox & Wyman Ltd,
London, Reading and Fakenham

COMFORTING TREATS FOR AUTUMN DAYS

In this, the third in her series of four
seasonal cook-books, *TV Times* cookery
editor Kathie Webber provides a wealth of
tasty menus and recipes for Autumn.

Warming casseroles and stews, nourishing
vegetable dishes and delectable puddings are
staple Autumn fare, and Kathie gives us old
favourites as well as tempting newcomers.
She also has plenty of ideas for the two
special Autumn occasions – Hallowe'en and
Bonfire Night – that would make any party
go with a bang!

Also by Kathie Webber in Sphere Books:

Kathie Webber's Book of Spring Cooking
Kathie Webber's Book of Summer Cooking

Contents

Metric Measurements

Metric measurements may vary from recipe to recipe, and it is essential to follow *either* imperial or metric measures throughout any one recipe. It's perfectly possible to specify 8-oz quantities in two recipes and have one convert to 200 g and the other to 225 g; this is of particular importance with, for example, pastry, where exact quantities are necessary to achieve the correct flour/fat ratio.

Another discrepancy, you may think, occurs when I've specified larger metric amounts of food than one would normally buy by the pound or half-pound. Nowadays we ask for ½ lb of tomatoes, not 7 oz (which may be what we want for a recipe) and in future we shall probably ask for a ½ kilo (kg) rather than 450 g. Half a kilo is a little more than 1 lb, but where the slight difference in weight won't alter the recipe I've given a metric quantity as you'd buy it.

Introduction

Autumn is the third season in the cook's calendar and the third book in this series, written specially to help you enjoy foods at their best. Although you might have decided it was autumn ages ago because it's been so cold, or are deciding to put off autumn for a while longer as you enjoy the summer pursuits and pastimes, the cook's year goes on. Autumn for us begins in September with the pickling and chutney-making, continues through October and into November with the party season which flickers briefly with Guy Fawkes night, then explodes into real candle-power towards the end of the month and the beginning of December when all the best of the family celebrating takes place. But more of that in the winter book. For now, a glimpse of what autumn has in store, beginning with the greengrocers.

I've given potatoes real status in this book, with a chapter of their own. Originally I was going to include them with the other vegetables but when I began to look into the subject, and turned up more and more ways of cooking them and recipes from all over the world, I decided that they made a marvellous subject in their own right. I particularly like the recipes for sweet dishes and cakes using potatoes as an ingredient. These are moist and enormously successful, with a light texture. It seems the most unlikely thing to add potatoes to a rich chocolate cake, but since testing this recipe it's become a favourite; even in a family of chocolate-cake lovers and connoisseurs like mine, the cake isn't around long enough to even think of turning it into a trifle.

All the new season's crop of root vegetables is lifted about this time, and though most of them are around all year, they're especially good when young and fresh. Serve them plain-boiled or mashed; turnips with butter and pepper are an excellent accompaniment to the weekend roast. New-season's beetroot should be spiced. I like to boil them myself because I always find them too soft when I buy them ready-cooked from the greengrocer. Even if they go into the spiced vinegar with a little resistance in each slice as you bite, a few weeks' storage cures that perfectly. New leeks and new onions, without which all our casseroles, stews, pies and soups would be very dull, are also marvellous on their own. They make very pleasing supper dishes, tasty and filling. When the frost gets at the celery it will be crisper, but at least it's in the shops now, looking and tasting fresh. You might well find celeriac in your shop, too, and not know what it is. Greengrocers have not been too good at labelling their produce – eating apples are rarely named, though lately I have noticed an improvement in this. Celeriac looks like a darker, large turnip with a crinkled, tough-looking skin and is good to eat. Remember, though, that it needs to be put into water made acid with lemon juice just as soon as it's prepared because it quickly turns brown – more quickly than apple discolours when cut and left.

It's an in-between season for fish, with all the perennials around but little to jump in and take the place of the summer varieties. Hake and herrings are the particular news of the autumn months, both relatively cheap and not eaten as much as they deserve. In this chapter I've also looked at whelks, eels, herring roes, kippers and smoked haddock and included some good fish pies – and a recipe for perfect fish and chips.

The butchers' shops are where the greatest change has taken place over the last couple of months. Grouse, pheasant and partridge should all be plentiful. While game is never cheap, it's most expensive at the beginning of each bird's season – August 12th for grouse and September 1st for pheasant and partridge. Game is not something that the majority of us have the money or the taste for but it is delicious, and I have included the classic roasting methods for these three birds, together with their accompaniments and number of servings. It's the one kind of present that's likely to nonplus simply because there aren't that many books which describe exact cooking procedures. Rounding out the game section is a small piece on venison, hare and, although it's available all year round, rabbit. Pigeons, also available all year round, are at their best in early autumn and make good eating. But the bulk of this chapter goes to the recipes in which we're most interested at this time of the year – casseroles, stews, and other ways with all the everyday meats.

Rice has no season but because it goes so well with curries and casseroles, I've given it a chapter in this book. Like potatoes, it's the main foodstuff of an enormous number of people in the world so there are many interesting ways to use it besides boiling it. I've included both sweet and savoury dishes here, an interesting cross-section of what the world eats.

After a summer of light little froths of whipped fruits and cream for dessert, puddings now begin to take on more substance. Most of those here are based on the fruits in great abundance now – apples, pears, blackberries, the plum and its family. There are lots of lovely dishes which are fun to make as well as good to eat, including Chinese Toffee Apples – which you may have eaten in a Chinese restaurant and thought you'd never be able to cook at home; now you can.

When the first real autumn day comes the light is almost luminous, making everything appear spacious and clean. But soon the leaves begin to turn brilliant shades of yellow and red, and slowly they build up on the ground, a whole collection stuck down with a fine misty moistness which is quite different to the spring and summer rains. That's the time to rush home, make lots of thick toast, pile on honey, home-made preserves, dripping or butter and sit and enjoy the warmth indoors.

Although I always think of teatimes in Autumn as particularly cosy, there are days when you want to serve thin bread and butter, good tea and the nicest pastries the baker can provide. I've included a special chapter for these occasions, in which I suggest that instead of nipping down to the baker's, you make your own selection of teatime cakes. All the favourites are here – cream horns, choux buns, chocolate boxes and Viennese tarts – and not difficult to make.

The freezer has real advantages for many of us, but there's still nothing which can replace the traditional pre-serving methods for jam, chutney and pickle-making. Most of the day-to-day preserves for the rest of the year are made in autumn. There are onions to pickle, mixed vegetables to brine, plums to stone for jam and hedgerow fruits to collect for jams, jellies, drinks and syrups, many of which will make lovely presents.

Both the occasions for parties in this season – Hallowe'en and Guy Fawkes night – call for chunkier, heartier food than summer feasts – good stout dishes like lasagne, curry, bangers and mash and chicken drumsticks, which can be eaten with the fingers or, at most, with a fork. All those included here are enormously enjoyed either out-of-doors round a bonfire or indoors, should Guy Fawkes night be rained out once again.

This, then, is the autumn book – full of good and nourish-ing foods to cook and eat. It's the best thing in the world at this time of the year to come home to a warm and cosy house – so make it a house that's full of delicious aromas that promise great meals.

Potatoes

We all take potatoes for granted. I did until I began to look into the subject for this chapter. There are some cultures in the world which rely on rice as the cheap, readily-available and filling main ingredient for meals – China, Japan and India are three such countries and there are more in the Far East. But a vast number of people depend on the potato. From the cold northern areas in Russia through the tropical regions of North and South America to the temperate zones of New Zealand's tip, housewives are peeling and cooking this tuber.

In this country, we miss the full potential of the potato, sticking to boiling, mashing, roasting, chipping and occasionally topping a savoury pie with them. But recipes from all over the world show that we can use potatoes to make pastry, gooey chocolate cakes, puddings and cookies as well as pancakes, dumplings and tasty main courses. The culinary histories of most of these countries contain recipes using potatoes which have survived almost unchanged to this day and many of them are here, together with a note of their country of origin. Like me, you might not have realised how versatile a friend the potato is, but I guarantee you'll be pleasantly surprised as you browse through these ideas.

Boiled Potatoes

675 g (1½ lb) potatoes	1 egg yolk (optional)
salt	5 ml (1 level teaspoon)
pepper	parsley, chopped
25 g (1 oz) butter (optional)	

Peel the potatoes, rinse them in cold water and cut them into even-sized pieces, about the size of a large plum. Put them in cold water, add a good pinch of salt and bring to the boil. Cover the pan and cook them for 20 minutes or until soft but not breaking. Drain well and return the pan to the heat for a minute to toss the potatoes and dry them thoroughly. Sprinkle with pepper and serve; or mash them with a fork or a masher until they are smooth and fluffy, beating in the butter and egg yolk, if liked, and seasoning the mash with a little salt and some pepper. Sprinkle with the parsley to serve.

Serves 4–6

Roast Potatoes

675 g (1½ lb) old potatoes, peeled	dripping or oil
	salt and pepper

Cut the potatoes into even-sized pieces, each one about the size of a small lemon. Melt enough dripping in a roasting tin, or pour in enough oil, to just cover the base. Heat the tin in an oven set at 220°C(425°F)/Gas 7 then add the potatoes, turning them to coat with fat. Season them with salt and pepper and roast the potatoes for 1–1½ hours. Turn them several times during the cooking so that they brown on all sides. Drain them on kitchen paper, sprinkle with a little extra salt and serve.

Serves 6

Chips

675 g (1½ lb) old potatoes,   lard or oil
  peeled   salt

Cut the peeled potatoes into 1.25-cm (½-in) slices, then cut each slice into 1.25-cm (½-in) sticks. Leave the chips to soak in a bowl of cold water to remove excess starch. Melt enough lard in a chip pan or saucepan to fill it to the half-way mark, or pour in enough oil. Don't fill it more than half-full because if you do there's a great danger of the fat bubbling over when the chips are put in. Drain the chips and dry them thoroughly on a tea towel. Make sure they are dry because drops of water will make the fat spit all over the place. Heat the lard until it gives off a blue haze. If you are cooking with oil, keep testing the temperature with a chip until it will rise, sizzling, covered with bubbles. Don't heat until the oil has a haze over it, because this will mean it's burning. On a thermometer, cook chips at 199°C(390°F). Gently lower in enough chips to fill the pan but be careful to allow them enough room in which to move about as they cook. Keep the heat high to bring the chips and fat back to the right temperature, then when they are sizzling, turn down the controls to maintain that heat. Cook for about 20 minutes or until the chips are crisp and golden brown. Remove from the fat, allowing them to drip for a few seconds, then turn on to absorbent kitchen paper to drain completely. Sprinkle with salt and serve.

Serves 4–6

Crisps (Game Chips)

450 g (1 lb) old potatoes,   lard or oil
  peeled   salt

Choose even-sized potatoes and slice them very thinly on a
mandolin, or the side of a suitable grater. (It's a tedious and
difficult job to slice them thinly enough with a knife.) Soak
the crisps in a bowl of cold water to remove excess starch,
then drain them and dry them on a tea towel, making sure
they are dry. Heat the lard or oil, exactly as described for
chips and to the same temperature, and fry the crisps in
batches for about 3 minutes per batch or until they are crisp
and a pale gold colour. Remove from the pan and allow
to drip for a few seconds, then drain them thoroughly on
kitchen paper. Sprinkle with salt. Crisps can be stored in an
air-tight tin for a while so it's possible to make a batch for a
party before the day.

Serves 6–8

Jacket Potatoes

8 large potatoes

Butter filling:
100 g (4 oz) butter
salt and pepper

Cream cheese filling:
225 g (8 oz) cream cheese
30 ml (2 level tablespoons)
  thyme, chopped
10 ml (2 level teaspoons)
  parsley, chopped
salt and pepper

Soured cream filling:
142-g (5-oz) carton soured
  cream
60 ml (4 level tablespoons)
  chives, snipped
salt and pepper

Mayonnaise filling:
125 ml ($\frac{1}{4}$ pint)
  mayonnaise, see page 44
1 clove garlic, crushed
15 ml (1 level tablespoon)
  tarragon, chopped

Scrub the potatoes and wrap each one in a piece of foil to

enclose it completely. Bake the potatoes in the oven at 190°C(375°F)/Gas 5 or at the sides of a barbecue for at least 1 hour or until they feel soft when squeezed. Open the foil, make a long cut in each potato and fill with one of the fillings.

For the butter filling, divide the butter into 8 pieces and add one with salt and pepper to each potato. Beat the cream cheese with the thyme, parsley and salt and pepper and divide between the potatoes. Whisk the soured cream with the chives and salt and pepper and spoon into the potatoes. Or if you want to use the mayonnaise filling, mix the mayonnaise with the clove of garlic and the tarragon and divide between the potatoes.

If you want to make up the four fillings, quarter the quantities and divide each filling between 2 potatoes.

Serves 8

Potato Croquettes

450 g (1 lb) old potatoes,
  mashed
25 g (1 oz) butter
2 large eggs
5 ml (1 level teaspoon)
  parsley, chopped

salt and pepper
50 g (2 oz) fresh white
  breadcrumbs
oil for deep frying

You need to make fresh mashed potato for this dish and to mash it really finely, beating in the butter. Beat the eggs well and add a very little to the potatoes with the parsley and seasoning. Allow to cool, then form the mixture into 8 cork shapes. Add 5 ml (1 teaspoon) cold water to the remaining egg and dip each croquette in egg to coat it, then roll it in the breadcrumbs. Shake off the excess and leave them on a baking tray to dry. Then repeat the egg and crumb coating as this helps prevent the croquettes breaking during cooking. Heat the oil to 185°C(365°F) or until a 2.5-cm (1-in) cube of bread will brown in 1 minute. Lower in the croquettes and fry them for about 5 minutes or until they are golden brown. Drain on kitchen paper and serve at once.

Serves 4

Sauté Potatoes

450 g (1 lb) potatoes,
  peeled
salt
50 g (2 oz) butter

15 ml (1 tablespoon) oil
pepper
5 ml (1 level teaspoon)
  chives, snipped

Cut the potatoes into even-sized chunks and boil them in salted water for 15 minutes or until they are just short of tender. Drain them well. When cool enough to handle, cut them into 0.5-cm (¼-in) thick slices. Heat the butter and oil in a large frying pan and fry the potato slices until they are crisp and golden on one side, then turn them and cook the other side in the same way. Drain on kitchen paper and fry the second batch if necessary, keeping the others hot. Sprinkle with a little salt and pepper and the chives and serve.

Serves 4

Pommes Duchesse

450 g (1 lb) potatoes,
  boiled
50 g (2 oz) butter

1 large egg
salt and pepper
ground mace

Drain the cooked potatoes well and push them through a sieve to make a smooth purée. Beat in the butter, egg, salt and pepper and a little ground mace to flavour them. Spoon the mixture into a large piping bag fitted with a 1.25-cm

($\frac{1}{2}$-in) star pipe and pipe rosettes about 5 cm (2 in) high on a
well-greased baking tray. Bake them at 200°C(400°F)/Gas 6
for about 25 minutes or until they are golden brown.

Serves 4

Pommes Lyonnaise

225 g ($\frac{1}{2}$ lb) onions, sliced salt
30 ml (2 tablespoons) oil 15 ml (1 level tablespoon)
450 g (1 lb) sauté potatoes parsley, chopped
 (see page 16)

Fry the onions in the oil slowly for about 10 minutes or until
they are golden brown. Layer the potatoes in a serving dish
with the well-drained onions, sprinkling each layer with a
little salt. Top with the parsley and serve hot.

Serves 4–6

Pommes Anna

75 g (3 oz) butter salt and pepper
675 g (1$\frac{1}{2}$ lb) potatoes,
 peeled

Thickly butter a round 15-cm (6-in) cake tin with a fixed
base, using 15 g ($\frac{1}{2}$ oz) of the butter. Line the base of the tin
with greaseproof paper and grease the paper with a little
more butter. Cut the potatoes into thin slices and wash
them in plenty of cold water to remove some of the starch.
Dry the slices on a clean tea towel and put a layer in the tin.
Beat the remaining butter until it is very soft and easy to
spread. Season the potatoes with salt and pepper and spread
with a little of the butter. Continue layering in this way,
making the top layer a coating of the remaining butter.

Cover the tin with foil and cook it at 190°C(375°F)/Gas 5
for about 1 hour. Check the potatoes towards the end of the
cooking time, adding a little more butter if they seem dry.
Test by pushing a thin skewer through the potato layers.
Turn out of the tin on to a plate to serve.

Serves 6

Sugar-browned Potatoes (Denmark)

450 g (1 lb) potatoes,
  peeled
40 g (1½ oz) granulated
  sugar
25 g (1 oz) butter
15 ml (1 tablespoon) hot
  water

Choose small even-sized potatoes for this dish, or cut large
round balls from old potatoes using a potato-ball cutter.
Cook the potatoes in water for about 5 minutes. Heat the
sugar in a heavy frying pan over a gentle heat until it becomes a golden brown syrup, then add the butter and water
and stir well. Drain the potatoes very well, add them to the
pan and gently stir them round while cooking until they
become an even golden brown all over. This should take
about 10 minutes.

Serves 4

Punchnep (Wales)

450 g (1 lb) potatoes,
  peeled
450 g (1 lb) white turnips,
  peeled
salt
50 g (2 oz) butter
pepper
125 ml (¼ pint) double
  cream, warmed

Cut the potatoes and turnips into even-sized pieces and cook

them separately in boiling, salted water. When soft enough
to mash, drain them well and mash them separately, or push
them through a sieve. Mix together, beating in the butter,
plenty of salt and a lot of freshly ground white pepper.
Spoon the mixture into a bowl and smooth the surface.
Make small holes all over the surface with the handle of a
wooden spoon, each hole about 2.5 cm (1 in) deep. Fill them
with the warmed cream.

Serves 8

Colcannon (Ireland)

450 g (1 lb) old potatoes, peeled	2 rashers fat bacon, chopped
salt	1 large onion, finely chopped
225 g (½ lb) cabbage, shredded	pepper

Cut the potatoes into even-sized pieces and cook them in
salted water for about 20 minutes or until soft enough to
mash. Cook the cabbage in boiling salted water for 5
minutes. Drain and chop it. Drain the potatoes well and
mash them until smooth. Fry the bacon gently in a frying
pan without adding any fat, then add the chopped onion
after 2 minutes' cooking and cook both for 5 minutes. Mix
with the potato, adding the cabbage and season well with
salt and pepper. Transfer the mixture to an ovenproof pie
dish and bake it at 190°C(375°F)/Gas 5 for about 20
minutes.

Serves 4–6

Bubble and Squeak

325 g (¾ lb) potatoes,
  mashed
325 g (¾ lb) cabbage,
  cooked

salt and pepper
25 g (1 oz) dripping

Mix the mashed left-over potatoes with the cooked cabbage, chopping the cabbage a little if necessary and seasoning the mixture with a little salt and plenty of pepper. Heat half the dripping in a large frying pan, add the potato mixture and smooth it into a flat cake to fill the pan. Cook it slowly for 10 minutes until it is brown underneath, then put a plate upside down over the frying pan and turn the pan over so the bubble and squeak drops on to the plate. Heat the remaining dripping and slide the potato cake back into the pan. Cook again for 10 minutes until the second side is brown. Cut into wedges and serve.

Serves 4–6

Champ (Ireland)

675 g (1½ lb) potatoes,
  peeled
salt and pepper
165 ml (11 tablespoons)
  milk

5 ml (1 level teaspoon)
  chives, chopped
25 g (1 oz) butter

Cut the potatoes into even-sized pieces and cook them in salted water for 20 minutes. Drain and mash the potatoes until smooth, adding salt and pepper. Bring the milk and the chives to the boil and gradually beat this mixture into the potatoes until the whole thing is light and fluffy. Serve very hot, piling the potato on to plates and making a small well in the top of each mound. Add a knob of butter to each well.

Serves 4–6

Baked Potato Purée (Russia)

450 g (1 lb) potatoes,
  boiled
125 ml ($\frac{1}{4}$ pint) milk
1 large egg
25 g (1 oz) butter, melted

2 large onions, chopped
30 ml (2 tablespoons) oil
salt and pepper
125 ml ($\frac{1}{4}$ pint) soured
  cream

Sieve the potatoes then beat in the milk, egg and butter.
Fry the onions in the oil for 5 minutes until they are soft but
not coloured. Layer the potato purée and the onions in an
ovenproof dish, sprinkling each layer with salt and pepper
and finishing with potatoes. Spread the soured cream over
the top and bake the dish at 180°C(350°F)/Gas 4 for about
30–40 minutes.

Serves 4–6

Boxty (Ireland)

1 kg ($2\frac{1}{4}$ lb) potatoes,
  peeled
salt
30 ml (2 level tablespoons)
  plain flour

5 ml (1 level teaspoon)
  baking powder

Reserve 1 large potato and cut the rest into small pieces.
Cook them in salted water for 20 minutes or until soft
enough to mash. Drain well and mash until smooth. Grate
the raw potato into a tea towel, then wring out the liquid.
Beat the grated potato into the mash with a good pinch of
salt. Sift the flour with the baking powder and mix it into
the potatoes. Turn the dough on to a lightly-floured board
and roll it out to a 1.25-cm ($\frac{1}{2}$-in) thickness, keeping the dough
a good round shape with your hands. Cut the round into
quarters. Grease a griddle or a very heavy frying pan with a
lard paper and add the potato quarters. Cook them slowly

for 40–45 minutes, turning them once, until they are nicely browned on both sides. Serve with bacon and eggs in the morning or with butter and jam for tea.

Serves 4

Potato Cheese Soufflé

450 g (1 lb) potatoes, boiled
175 g (7 oz) Cheddar cheese, grated
4 large eggs, separated

25 g (1 oz) butter
30 ml (2 tablespoons) milk
10 ml (1 level dessertspoon) chives, snipped
salt and pepper

Push the potatoes through a sieve and mix them with the cheese, egg yolks and butter. (If the potatoes are hot, the butter will melt; if they are cold, cream the butter until it is very soft before adding it to the mixture). Beat in the milk and snipped chives, and season with salt and pepper. Whisk the egg whites until they form soft peaks and fold them into the potato mixture. Transfer at once to a greased 18-cm (7-in) soufflé dish and bake at 220°C(425°F)/Gas 7 for 30–35 minutes or until the soufflé is well risen and golden brown.

Serves 4

Potato Soufflé (Holland)

900 g (2 lb) potatoes,
  boiled
125 ml ($\frac{1}{4}$ pint) double
  cream
50 g (2 oz) butter

4 large eggs, separated
salt and pepper
5 ml (1 level teaspoon)
  ground cinnamon

Sieve the potatoes to make them smooth. Gently heat the cream with the butter until the butter has melted, then beat this mixture into the potatoes with the egg yolks, salt and pepper and ground cinnamon for seasoning. Stiffly whisk the egg whites, fold them in quickly but lightly and, working fast, turn the mixture into 2 greased 15-cm (6-in) soufflé dishes. Bake at 150°C(300°F)/Gas 2 for about 45 minutes but don't disturb the soufflé while it cooks. Serve with a tomato sauce (see page 25), or as a vegetable with a main course.

Serves 8

Potato Pastry

100 g (4 oz) potatoes,
  boiled
125 g (5 oz) plain flour
75 g (3 oz) butter

5 ml (1 level teaspoon)
  baking powder
pinch of salt

Push the potatoes through a sieve to make sure they are very smooth, then mix with the flour. Cream the butter until it is very soft, and blend in the potato mixture, baking powder and salt and mix well. Turn the dough on to a lightly-floured board and knead it lightly. Roll out the pastry and use to make the top and bottom crust of a 20-cm (8-in) plate savoury pie.

Serves 4–8

Oatcakes

450 g (1 lb) potatoes,   5 ml (1 level teaspoon) salt
  boiled   milk to mix
150 g (6 oz) pinhead
  oatmeal

Push the freshly boiled potatoes through a sieve, then stir in
the oatmeal and salt. The dough should be stiff, so only add
a little milk if it's dry and unworkable. Turn on to a lightly-
floured board and roll it to an 0.25-cm ($\frac{1}{8}$-in) thickness. Cut
the dough into large rounds, using a saucer for size. Prick
them all over with a fork and cook them in a heavy frying
pan or on a griddle, lightly greasing it each time. Turn each
oatcake when the underside has light brown spots on it.
Serve buttered, for breakfast or supper.

Makes 8–10

Potato Pancakes

100 g (4 oz) plain flour   30 ml (2 level tablespoons)
good pinch of salt   onion, grated
250 ml ($\frac{1}{2}$ pint) milk   450 g (1 lb) potatoes,
2 large eggs   peeled
25 g (1 oz) butter   15 g ($\frac{1}{2}$ oz) lard

Sift the flour and salt into a bowl. Whisk the milk with the
eggs and gradually beat it into the flour. Heat the butter in a
frying pan and fry the onion for 5 minutes or until soft but
not coloured. Add the onion to the batter, then grate in the
potatoes, working quickly to prevent the pieces browning.
Use at once. Heat a frying pan and grease it well with a little
of the lard. Drop some of the potato mixture in small rounds
in the pan and fry for about 2–3 minutes, turning them once,
until they are golden on both sides. Grease the pan again
and fry more pancakes, keeping the cooked ones hot until

all the batter is used. If you have a small omelette pan, 15 cm (6 in) in diameter, make large pancakes. Top small ones with a spoonful of a savoury mixture such as smoked haddock in a white sauce, and roll the large pancakes. A savoury mince makes a good filling, as does a mild curry made from left-over roast meat.

Serves 4

Potato Dumplings (France)

225 g (8 oz) potatoes, boiled
75 g (3 oz) self-raising flour
1 small egg or ½ an egg, beaten

pinch of dried mixed herbs
salt

Push the potatoes through a sieve to make a smooth purée, then work in the flour, egg and mixed herbs. Blend very well and shape the mixture into small balls, using a little flour, but only if really necessary. Bring a large pan of water to the boil, add a pinch of salt and the dumplings and simmer them, covered, for 8–10 minutes. Remove with a draining spoon when they are cooked. Serve on top of any stew or casserole or as a pudding (omitting the herbs) with jam or a fruit sauce.

Serves 4

Potato Quenelles (France)

450 g (1 lb) potatoes, boiled
1 large egg yolk
pinch of ground nutmeg
salt and pepper
25 g (1 oz) butter, melted
500 ml (1 pint) chicken stock

Tomato sauce:
450 g (1 lb) tomatoes, skinned
1 small onion, chopped
25 g (1 oz) butter
15 ml (1 tablespoon) oil
salt and pepper
5 ml (1 level teaspoon) fresh basil, chopped

Push the freshly boiled potatoes through a sieve and beat in the egg yolk, nutmeg, salt and pepper and melted butter. Allow the mixture to cool. Heat the stock almost to boiling point, then take up one heaped teaspoon of the mixture for each quenelle and carefully lower it into the stock. Poach them, a few at a time, very gently for 4–5 minutes. Drain them well in a sieve.

Meanwhile, chop the tomatoes and put them in a pan with the onion, butter, oil, salt and pepper and basil and simmer the mixture for 30 minutes until it forms a thick sauce. Taste for seasoning and pour over the well-drained quenelles.

Serves 2–4

Rösti (Switzerland)

1 kg (2 lb) potatoes, peeled   pinch of salt
65 g (2½ oz) butter   45 ml (3 tablespoons) oil
1 large onion, finely
   chopped

Boil the potatoes for 10 minutes and drain well. Heat 40 g (1½) oz butter in a pan and fry the onion gently until it is soft but not coloured. Grate the potatoes into long shreds when they are cool enough to handle and sprinkle them with a little salt. Heat the remaining butter with the oil in a large frying pan and when hot add half the potatoes. Pat them into a flat cake, then cover them with the onion. Add the remaining potato shreds, again patting them flat, and fry the cake for about 8 minutes. When the bottom is golden brown, put a plate upside down over the frying pan and turn the pan over so the rösti drops on to the plate. Slide it back into the pan and continue cooking for another 8–10 minutes or until the underside is golden brown also.

Rösti is also made in Switzerland with a bacon filling. For

this, fry 65 g (2½ oz) chopped bacon in its own fat and spread over the potatoes as already described for the onions.

Serves 4–6

Jansson's Temptation (Sweden)

450 g (1 lb) old potatoes, peeled
65 g (2½ oz) butter
30 ml (2 tablespoons) oil
3 large onions, thinly sliced
16 anchovy fillets, drained
pepper
30 ml (2 level tablespoons) fine breadcrumbs, dried
125 ml (¼ pint) double cream
125 ml (¼ pint) milk

Cut the potatoes into thin slices about 0.5 cm (¼ in) thick and put them in a bowl of cold water. Heat 25 g (1 oz) butter with the oil in a large frying pan and fry the onions slowly for about 10 minutes until they are soft but not coloured. Use 15 g (½ oz) butter to grease a large soufflé dish or ovenproof casserole. Drain the potatoes well, dry them on a tea towel and put a layer in the bottom of the dish. Add a layer of onion and some anchovies and continue layering, sprinkling pepper on each layer and finishing with potatoes. Top with the breadcrumbs and dot with the remaining butter. Heat the cream and milk to simmering point and pour it into the potato layer, down the side of the dish. Bake at 200°C (400°F)/Gas 6 for about 45 minutes. When ready the liquid should have been absorbed and the potatoes will be tender when tested with a skewer.

Serves 4–6

Potatoes with Cheese and Tomato Sauce (Colombia)

Cheese and tomato sauce:
25 g (1 oz) butter
1 small onion, finely
  chopped
4 spring onions, prepared
4 large tomatoes, skinned
75 ml (5 tablespoons)
  double cream

5 ml (1 level teaspoon)
  ground coriander
pinch of ground oregano
pinch of ground cumin
salt and pepper
25 g (1 oz) mozzarella
  cheese, grated
12 small potatoes, boiled

In Colombia, this dish is made with a cheese unknown in
Britain. Mozzarella is the best substitute and combines well
with the other flavours. Melt the butter in a frying pan and
when it is very hot add the chopped onion. Cut the spring
onions into 2.5-cm (1-in) lengths, including the green leaves.
Add to the pan and cook the onions for about 5 minutes or
until they are soft but not coloured. Scoop the seeds from
the tomatoes and use only the flesh for this recipe. Chop the
flesh roughly, add to the pan and cook, stirring, for 5
minutes. Add the cream, coriander, oregano, cumin and
salt and pepper and stir well. Grate the cheese into the pan,
stirring well after a few gratings, then continue adding the
cheese and stirring until the cheese has melted. Pour the
sauce at once over the freshly boiled potatoes and serve.

Serves 4

Deep-fried Potato and Chick Pea Snacks (India)

65 g (2½ oz) dried chick peas
tiny pinch of bicarbonate
  of soda
1 small onion, grated
1 large potato, grated
5 ml (1 level teaspoon)
  ground coriander

pinch of cayenne pepper
pinch of ground cumin
5 ml (1 level teaspoon) salt
oil for deep frying

You can only make this dish if you have a coffee grinder. Put some of the dried chick peas into the grinder and grind them to a powder. Tip out and repeat until you have turned them all into chick-pea flour. Mix this with the bicarbonate of soda and 60 ml (4 tablespoons) cold water. Grate in the onion and potato, then stir in the coriander, cayenne pepper, cumin and salt and mix well. Heat the oil to 177°C(350°F). Take up a spoonful of the batter and scrape it into the hot oil using another spoon. Fry for 6–7 minutes until they are golden, then remove them with a draining spoon and drain them on kitchen paper. Cook the rest of the batter in the same way. Serve as a snack.

Makes about 8

Potato Pudding (Portugal)

450 g (1 lb) potatoes, boiled	75 g (3 oz) plain flour
2 large eggs	oil for deep frying
50 g (2 oz) caster sugar	50 g (2 oz) almonds, finely chopped

Sieve the potatoes to make them smooth, then allow to cool. Separate 1 egg, then beat in the whole egg, egg yolk and sugar. Mix in the flour. Whisk the egg white stiffly and fold it in. Form the mixture into small balls. Heat the oil to 185°C(365°F) or until a 2.5-cm (1-in) cube of bread will brown in 1 minute, then fry the potato balls until they are golden brown on all sides. Drain well on kitchen paper and serve sprinkled with the almonds and, if liked, with cream.

Serves 4–6

Sweet Potato Dumplings (Germany)

50 g (2 oz) butter	salt
25 g (1 oz) fresh white	ground nutmeg
breadcrumbs	100 g (4 oz) plum jam,
1 kg (2 lb) potatoes, sieved	sieved
125 g (5 oz) plain flour	50 g (2 oz) caster sugar
1 large egg, separated	ground cinnamon
1 egg yolk	

Heat the butter in a frying pan and fry the crumbs, stirring them all the time, until they are golden brown. Remove from the heat and allow to cool. Mix the potatoes with the flour, then beat in the egg yolks one at a time. Add a good pinch of salt and nutmeg and beat until you have a smooth dough. Cover the bowl with a piece of foil and put the dough in the fridge for an hour.

Sprinkle the underside of a large Swiss roll tin with a small handful of flour, spreading it well. Turn the dough on to the tin and using a floured rolling pin, roll the dough to the size of the tin, approximately 30 by 38 cm (12 by 15 in). If the dough becomes sticky and too difficult to handle, put it back in the fridge and chill it again. Cut the rolled dough into 7.5-cm (3-in) squares using a ruler and a pastry wheel or knife. Put 5 ml (1 level teaspoon) of the jam in the middle of each square. Lightly beat the egg white and brush a little on all the edges of the pastry dough. Fold each square in half diagonally to make triangles and pinch the edges well to seal. Bring a large pan of water to the boil, add a good 5 ml (1 level teaspoon) salt and add 3 or 4 dumplings at a time, moving them around in the water at first to prevent them sticking to each other and the pan. Simmer gently for 3–4 minutes or until they rise to the top of the pan. Remove with a draining spoon and arrange them on a heated dish while you cook 3 or 4 more. Mix the caster sugar with a good pinch of cinnamon, then taste a little and add more sugar or cinnamon if necessary. When the dumplings are cooked, sprinkle them all with the sugar and fried breadcrumbs and serve at once.

Serves 4–6

Steamed Pudding

225 g (8 oz) potatoes,
  boiled
pinch of salt
1 large egg, beaten
25 g (1 oz) Demerara sugar

50 g (2 oz) butter, melted
75 g (3 oz) mixed dried fruit
1 small lemon
15 ml (1 tablespoon)
  brandy

Push the freshly boiled potatoes through a sieve, then beat in the salt, egg, sugar, butter and dried fruit. Finely grate the rind from the lemon and squeeze out and strain the juice. Add to the bowl with the brandy and mix well. Turn the mixture into a greased 1-litre (1¾-pint) pudding basin and cover with greased greaseproof paper or foil. Steam for 1½ hours and serve with cream.

Serves 6

Potato Apple Cake (Ireland)

450 g (1 lb) potatoes,
  boiled
40 g (1½ oz) butter
5 ml (1 level teaspoon)
  caster sugar
3 ml (½ level teaspoon)
  ground cinnamon

100 g (4 oz) plain flour,
  sifted
2 large cooking apples,
  thinly sliced
15 g (½ oz) Demerara sugar

Push the freshly boiled potatoes through a sieve and beat in 25 g (1 oz) butter, the caster sugar, cinnamon and flour to make a smooth, though rather soft, dough. Roll it on a

lightly-floured board into 2 thick rounds, one slightly larger
than the other. Transfer the smaller round to a greased
baking tray. Cover it with sliced apples and moisten the edge
of the dough with cold water. Cover with the large round
and pinch the edges together between finger and thumb
to seal them. Make a large cross in the top crust, then bake
it at 180°C(350°F)/Gas 4 for about 45 minutes until the
cake is brown and the apples are soft. Remove from the oven
and cut around the cross and lift out this circular lid. Thinly
slice the remaining butter and spread it over the apples,
then sprinkle with the Demerara sugar. Put the lid back on
and return the cake to the oven for 1 minute. Serve at once.

Serves 4

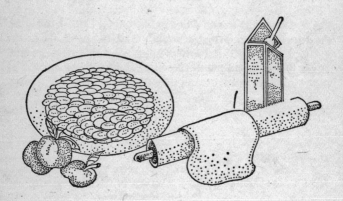

Chocolate Cake

75 g (3 oz) potatoes,
   boiled
100 g (4 oz) butter
150g (6 oz) caster sugar
40 g (1½ oz) plain
   chocolate, melted
2 large eggs, beaten
150 g (6 oz) self-raising
   flour, sifted
pinch of salt
milk to mix

Filling:
75 g (3 oz) butter

150 g (6 oz) icing sugar,
   sifted
15 ml (1 level tablespoon)
   cocoa, sifted
30 ml (2 tablespoons) warm
   water

Icing:
125 g (5 oz) icing sugar,
   sifted
1 large egg
25 g (1 oz) plain chocolate,
   melted
25 g (1 oz) butter

Sieve the freshly cooked potatoes to make them smooth.
Cream the butter and sugar until the mixture is light and
fluffy, then beat in the sieved potato and melted chocolate.
Stir in the eggs, fold in the flour and salt and mix to a soft
dropping consistency with milk. Turn the mixture into a
greased 20-cm (8-in) tin and bake at 190°C(375°F)/Gas 5
for 45–50 minutes or until the cake is well risen and the
centre springs back when you press it lightly. Allow to cool
for a couple of minutes, then turn the cake on to a wire rack
to cool completely.

Cream the butter for the filling until it is very soft, then
gradually beat in the icing sugar. Blend the cocoa with the
warm water to a smooth cream and when it has cooled,
beat it into the butter and sugar. Cut the cake into two layers
and sandwich it together again with the chocolate filling.

Put all the ingredients for the icing into a large bowl and
stand the bowl over a pan of gently simmering water. Make
sure the base of the bowl is above the water. Whisk the icing
until it is thick, fluffy and glossy. Spread it quickly over the
cake and down the sides, then leave it to set.

Serves 10

Potato Doughnuts

100 g (4 oz) plain flour,
  sifted
10 ml (2 level teaspoons)
  baking powder, sifted
50 g (2 oz) butter
50 g (2 oz) potatoes,
  boiled

pinch of ground nutmeg
½ large egg, beaten
oil for deep frying
caster sugar

Mix the sifted flour and baking powder in a large bowl and
rub in the butter. Sieve the freshly boiled potatoes to make a
smooth mixture, add to the bowl with the nutmeg and egg
and mix to form a stiff dough. Turn it on to a lightly-
floured board and roll it to a 1.25-cm (½-in) thickness. Using
plain cutters, cut 7.5-cm (3-in) rounds, then cut out the
middles using a 2.5-cm (1-in) cutter. Knead the centres
lightly, roll out again and cut more doughnuts, or simply
use the middles as they are to make tiny doughnut puffs.
Heat the oil to 182°C(360°F) or until a 2.5-cm (1-in) cube of
bread will brown in 1 minute. Add a few doughnuts at a
time and fry them for about 5 minutes, turning them over
when the underside is golden brown. Remove and drain on
kitchen paper while you fry the next batch. Sprinkle with
caster sugar and eat hot.

Makes 8

Nutty Potato Cookies

100 g (4 oz) butter
150 g (6 oz) caster sugar
1 large egg, beaten
150 g (6 oz) potatoes,
  boiled
225 g (8 oz) self-raising
  flour, sifted

50 g (2 oz) walnuts, finely
  chopped
15 ml (1 level tablespoon)
  clear honey

Cream the butter and caster sugar until the mixture is light and fluffy. Beat in the egg. Sieve the freshly boiled potatoes and stir them into the creamed mixture with the flour, nuts and honey. Using a 15 ml spoon (one tablespoon) scoop the mixture and push off the spoon into small rounds on greased baking trays. Bake at 200°C(400°F)/Gas 6 for about 15 minutes, or until they are golden. Remove and cool on a wire rack.

Makes 18

Vegetables

It's in autumn, when the first nippy days make us think of preparing a casserole again, that the root vegetables, which add so much flavour to our soups and stews, begin to appear. Most important is the onion which goes into just about everything savoury, lifting the taste as salt and pepper do; and like no seasoning, an absence of onion would make very dull meals. Onions are at their best new, firm and juicy; as time passes they'll lose a lot in storage, so make the most of them in the autumn months.

New turnips are in the shops, quite small at the moment, unblemished and really needing a bit of frost to bring out their best. In the north of England, leek shows take place and the winning vegetables are often 10-cm (4-in) in diameter, magnificent-looking specimens but lacking the flavour of the smaller more familiar varieties. My father, a would-be champion grower, once gave me his prized leek, disgraced after months of nurturing for not even receiving an honourable mention at the local show. It looked as if it would be the best thing I'd ever tasted but instead it disappointed. The old truism that produce too thin or too fat doesn't have the flavour of the medium-sized crops required no better demonstration.

Celery, also needing a touch of frost, is new season's and you could find celeriac in the shops. This is another of those knobbly-looking roots, so often not named in greengrocers, but well worth the trouble of asking for it, buying, peeling and rushing it into water made acid with lemon juice to prevent the celeriac discolouring. Beetroot are good now, and the first of the real winter vegetables – the cauliflower – appears.

Mashed Turnips

450 g (1 lb) turnips   ground nutmeg
salt   25 g (1 oz) butter
pepper

Cut off the roots and stems from the turnips and peel off the tough outer skin which will probably mean peeling quite thickly. Cut the turnips into even-sized chunks and cook

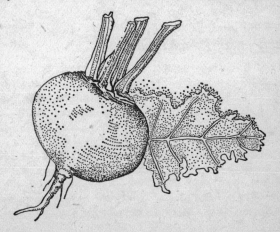

them in salted water for 15–25 minutes, depending on the age of the turnips. Drain well, return the turnips to the dry pan and steam them over a high heat for a minute or two, shaking the pan all the time to make sure they don't burn. Mash them well, adding salt, pepper and ground nutmeg for seasoning. Mash in the butter and serve hot.

Serves 4

Turnips in Cream

450 g (1 lb) young turnips,   142-g (5-oz) carton double
  peeled   cream
salt   pepper
40 g (1½ oz) butter

Cut the turnips into round slices, each about 1.25 cm (½ in) thick. Put them in a pan, just cover with cold salted water, and bring to the boil, then simmer them, covered, for 15 minutes. Drain. Add the butter and continue cooking gently, uncovered this time, until the turnips are soft. Now add the cream and season well with salt and pepper; as soon as the cream is hot serve the turnips.

Serves 4–6

Turnips with Breadcrumbs

450 g (1 lb) young turnips,   20 ml (2 level tablespoons)
  peeled   fresh white breadcrumbs
salt   15 ml (1 level tablespoon)
30 ml (2 tablespoons) good   parsley, chopped
  oil   1 clove garlic, chopped

Cut the turnips into even-sized pieces and cook them for 10 minutes in salted water. Drain well. Heat the oil in a frying pan, add the turnips and cook them slowly until they are tender. Shake them around from time to time to make sure they do not stick. Mix the breadcrumbs with the parsley and garlic, add to the pan and stir everything together to heat before serving.

Serves 4

Boiled Beetroot

0.5 kg (1 lb) small beetroot   salt

Rinse the beetroot to remove any earth and trim off the stems; leave about 2.5 cm (1 in) or the beetroot will 'bleed' while they are cooking. Trim off the roots, leaving a similar length. Bring a large pan of water to the boil, add a good pinch of salt and the beetroot and cook them for about 45 minutes to 1 hour. The time varies a lot and depends on the size and age of the beetroot but you can always tell when they are ready. Remove one from the pan and rub it gently with a finger. If the skin slips off easily, remove and drain them. Rub off the skin or scrape it off carefully with a knife, cutting off the stem and root pieces. Allow to cool and slice for a salad or serve hot, whole or sliced.

Serves 6

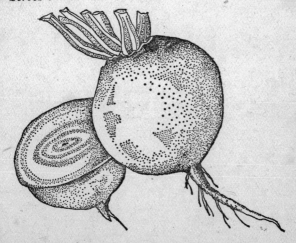

Beetroot in Béchamel Sauce

4 medium-sized beetroot, prepared	25 g (1 oz) plain flour
salt	250 ml (½ pint) milk
	salt and pepper
	ground nutmeg
Béchamel sauce:	5 ml (1 level teaspoon)
25 g (1 oz) butter	thyme, chopped

Bring a large pan of water to the boil, add a good pinch of salt and the beetroot and cook them for 45 minutes to 1 hour. Towards the end of the cooking time, make the béchamel sauce.

Melt the butter in a pan and stir in the flour. Cook for 1 minute, then remove from the heat and gradually stir in the milk. Return the pan to the heat and bring to the boil, stirring all the time, then cook the sauce for 2 minutes, stirring occasionally. Season with salt and pepper and some ground nutmeg.

Drain the beetroot and rub or scrape off the skins. Slice the beetroot thickly into a serving dish. Pour over the sauce, sprinkle with the thyme and serve.

Serves 4

Deep-fried Beetroot

2 medium-sized beetroot, cooked	45 ml (3 tablespoons) oil
	salt
Fritter batter:	1 large onion, thinly sliced
10 ml (1 level dessertspoon) baking powder	salt and pepper
	ground nutmeg
225 g (8 oz) plain flour, sifted	2 large egg whites, stiffly whisked
250 ml (½ pint) warm water	oil for deep frying

Rub off or scrape off the beetroot skins and slice the beetroot thinly.

Sift the baking powder with the flour, then mix in the warm water with the oil to make a thick smooth batter. Whisk in a good pinch of salt. Allow to stand for 1 hour.

Sandwich 2 slices of beetroot with 1 slice of onion and season each sandwich with salt and pepper and nutmeg. Heat the oil to 193°C(380°F). Fold the stiffly beaten egg whites into the batter and quickly dip in a few of the sandwiches. Fry in hot oil until golden brown and drain on kitchen paper. Keep hot while you fry the remainder.

Serves 4

Perfect Cauliflower

1 large cauliflower   pepper
salt

Rinse the cauliflower and cut off most of the coarse outside leaves; there is no need to remove them all. Cut off the thick stem close to the head. Make a criss-cross cut in the stem so that it cooks more quickly. You can leave the head whole or break it into small florets. Bring a pan of water to the boil and add a good pinch of salt. If you are cooking the whole cauliflower, put it – stalk down – into the boiling water and cook it, covered, for about 15 minutes or until the florets are tender but not mushy. Ideally the amount of water in the pan should be just high enough to boil the thick stem, leaving the florets above to be steamed. Remove and drain in a colander. You may break it into florets at this stage, but if you've cut it earlier, cook the florets in boiling salted water for about 10 minutes and drain them well in a colander. Sprinkle with pepper and serve.

Serves 4–6

Cauliflower Polonaise

1 whole cauliflower,
  cooked
25 g (1 oz) fresh white
  breadcrumbs

25 g (1 oz) butter
5 ml (1 level teaspoon)
  parsley, chopped

While the cauliflower cooks, fry the breadcrumbs in the hot butter in a frying pan, stirring them all the time, until they are golden and crisp. Drain the cauliflower well, put it in a serving dish and sprinkle it first with the breadcrumbs and then the parsley.

Serves 4–6

Cauliflower Fritters

Fritter batter:
225 g (8 oz) plain flour
pinch of salt
10 ml (2 level teaspoons)
    baking powder
1 large egg
1 large cauliflower,
    prepared

salt
90 ml (6 tablespoons) oil
juice of ½ lemon, strained
pepper
oil for deep frying

Sift the flour and salt with the baking powder into a large bowl. Make a well in the centre and add the egg, then gradually beat in 250 ml (½ pint) water to give a smooth batter which will coat the back of the wooden spoon well. Allow it to stand for 2 hours. Divide the cauliflower into florets and cook them in boiling salted water for about 15 minutes until tender but still firm. Drain them well and put them in a dish. Mix the oil with the lemon juice and a little salt and pepper and pour this over the hot cauliflower. Allow to stand for 1 hour. Heat the oil until a 2.5-cm (1-in) cube of bread will brown in 1 minute. On a thermometer, the temperature should read 196°C(385°F). Dip each floret into the batter and lower gently into the hot fat. Fry until golden brown, then remove and drain on kitchen paper while you fry the rest in the same way.

Serves 4–6

Celeriac with Melted Butter

325-g (¾-lb) root of celeriac
juice of 1 lemon, strained
salt

50 g (2 oz) unsalted butter
pepper

Choose a root which is about the size of a good Bramley apple. It should be firm and unblemished, rather like a turnip, although celeriac is a knobbly root with a rough skin. Cut off the roots and stems and peel it quickly, then, just as quickly, cut it into fairly thin slices. Drop them into a pan of cold water mixed with the lemon juice to prevent the slices browning. Remove the celeriac and bring the lemon water to the boil, adding a good pinch of salt. Add the celeriac and cook it for about 20–25 minutes or until tender. Drain it when it is as soft as you like your carrots. Melt the butter in a small pan, pour it over the celeriac, sprinkle with freshly ground pepper and serve.

Serves 4

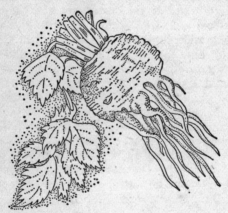

Celeriac Rémoulade

Mayonnaise:
1 large egg yolk
salt and pepper
5 ml (1 level teaspoon)
  Dijon mustard
125 ml (¼ pint) corn oil
white wine vinegar

1 root of celeriac, prepared
juice of 1 lemon, strained
5 ml (1 level teaspoon)
  parsley, chopped

Beat the egg yolk with a good pinch each of salt and pepper and the Dijon mustard. Continue beating well all the time and add the oil, 5 ml (1 teaspoon) at a time, beating well after each addition. When half the oil has been added, you will find you can add it a little more quickly without fear of curdling, but if it ever looks as though it might, stop adding oil and beat vigorously. Beat in a little white wine vinegar to thin it and check the seasoning.

Don't cut the celeriac until the mayonnaise is made and work quickly once you start, grating the peeled root straight into a bowl of water to which you've added the lemon juice. Bring a large pan of water to the boil and add 30 ml (2 tablespoons) of the vinegar. Drain the celeriac, add it to the pan, bring to the boil, then drain well. Tip it on to a tea towel and dry it thoroughly, then mix with the mayonnaise. Chill, and serve sprinkled with parsley.

Serves 4

Celeriac Purée

325-g (¾-lb) root of celeriac, peeled
salt
100 g (4 oz) potatoes, peeled
100 g (4 oz) butter
pepper
5 ml (1 level teaspoon) parsley, chopped

Cut the celeriac into 2.5-cm (1-in) cubes and drop them as you cut them into a pan of boiling salted water. Bring back to the boil and cook for 10 minutes. Roughly chop the potatoes and cook them in salted water for 15–20 minutes or until soft enough to mash. Drain the celeriac well, then melt 50 g (2 oz) butter in a pan, add the celeriac, cover the pan and cook very gently in the butter for 15–20 minutes or until it is tender, shaking the pan from time to time to prevent it sticking and burning. Push the celeriac through a nylon sieve into a bowl. Now sieve in the potatoes and beat the mixture well with the remaining butter, some salt and pepper and the parsley. Reheat gently and serve hot.

Serves 4–6

Good Celery

1 head of celery
salt
50 g (2 oz) butter
15 ml (1 level tablespoon)
   parsley, chopped

juice of ½ lemon, strained
pepper

Remove the outer stalks from a head of celery and use them for soup. Separate the stalks that are left and scrub them to remove any dirt. Cut off the leaves and save for soup and trim any root. Cut the stalks into 2.5-cm (1-in) slices. Bring a large pan of lightly salted water to the boil, add the celery strips and bring back to the boil, then simmer them for 15 minutes. Drain well, then melt the butter in the pan, add the celery, cover the pan and stew the strips for 10–15 minutes until tender but not soggy. Stir in the parsley and lemon juice and season with a little more salt and some freshly ground black pepper.

Serves 4

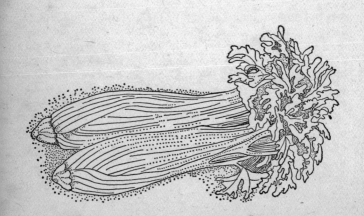

Braised Celery

1 head of celery, prepared
1 rasher of streaky bacon,
  chopped
1 small onion, chopped
250 ml (½ pint) chicken
  stock

salt and pepper
5 ml (1 level teaspoon)
  thyme, chopped

Choose a large head of celery and cut it into quarters down
its length and then again in halves across before washing.
Fry the bacon and onion together for 5 minutes. Transfer
them to an ovenproof dish large enough to hold the celery
when it is arranged on top. Pour on the stock and season
with salt and pepper. Sprinkle with the thyme, cover the dish
with a lid or foil and bake it at 160°C(325°F)/Gas 3 for
about 1½ hours. Drain well to serve.

Serves 4

Celery Chinese-style

1 small head of celery,
  prepared
225 g (½ lb) mushrooms
30 ml (2 tablespoons) oil
5 ml (1 level teaspoon) salt

30 ml (2 tablespoons) soy
  sauce
5 ml (1 level teaspoon)
  brown sugar

Cut the cleaned celery into 2.5-cm (1-in) lengths, slicing the
thicker stalks in half. Rinse the mushrooms, trim the stalks
and slice the mushrooms thickly. Heat the oil in a heavy
frying pan and stir-fry the mushrooms over a very high heat
for 1 minute. Add the celery pieces, salt, soy sauce and
brown sugar and stir-fry over the same high heat for about
5 minutes. The celery will still be fresh and crisp when ready
to serve.

Serves 4–6

Plain Cooked Leeks

675 g (1½ lb) leeks	5 ml (1 level teaspoon)
salt	parsley, chopped
pepper	

Cut off the roots and the tops of the leaves from the leeks. Remove any damaged and coarse outer leaves. Score each leek down its length quite deeply, and rinse thoroughly under running cold water to remove dirt and grit. You might find it necessary to cut them completely in half to achieve this. Cut each leek into 10-cm (4-in) lengths. Bring a large pan of salted water to the boil, add the leeks, cover the pan and simmer them for about 15 minutes, or until tender but not mushy. Drain well and arrange on a serving plate. Sprinkle with pepper and the parsley and serve.

Serves 4

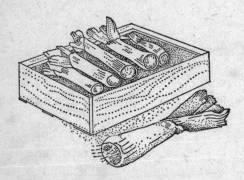

French Fried Leeks

675 g (1½ lb) leeks, prepared	4 medium-sized tomatoes, skinned
60 ml (4 tablespoons) olive oil	salt and pepper
1 clove garlic, chopped	5 ml (1 teaspoon) lemon juice, strained
1 bay leaf	

Cut the leeks into 2.5-cm (1-in) lengths. Heat the oil in a large frying pan. Cook the leeks with the garlic and bay leaf for about 20 minutes, covering the pan. Chop the tomatoes roughly, add them to the leeks and cook for another 5 minutes, stirring occasionally. Season well with salt and pepper, stir in the lemon juice and serve at once.

Serves 4–6

Poor Man's Asparagus

6 small leeks, prepared
salt

Vinaigrette:
60 ml (4 tablespoons) olive
  oil
15 ml (1 tablespoon) wine
  vinegar

salt and pepper

10 ml (1 level dessertspoon)
  parsley, chopped
1 egg, hard-boiled

Cut the washed leeks into 10-cm (4-in) lengths and cook them in boiling salted water for 15 minutes only. They should be tender but still slightly crisp. Drain well and when dry, arrange in a serving dish. Whisk together the oil, vinegar and salt and pepper and pour it over the hot leeks. Allow them to cool until they are just warm, then sprinkle with the parsley. Chop the egg, sprinkle on the leeks, and serve at once while the vegetables are still warm.

Serves 4

Simple Onions

4 large onions
salt

250 ml (½ pint) béchamel
  sauce (see page 40)

Cut off the roots and stalks from the onions and peel off the brown papery skins. Bring a large pan of salted water to the boil, add the onions and cook them, covered, for 30–40 minutes. They are nicest when still a little crisp, but the time they require will depend on their size. Drain them well, arrange them in a serving dish and coat with the béchamel sauce. Serve at once.

Serves 4

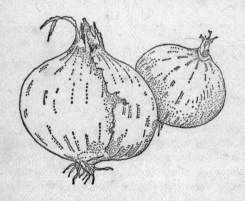

Onion Crisps

4 large onions, prepared   salt and pepper
60 ml (4 tablespoons) milk   oil for deep frying
25 g (1 oz) plain flour

Cut the onions into 0.5-cm ($\frac{1}{4}$-in) slices and separate the rings in each slice. Dip each ring first in the milk and then in the flour seasoned with a little salt and pepper. Shake off excess flour and fry them, a few at a time, in oil which has reached 193°C(380°F). (To test the oil without a thermo- meter, add one onion ring; if it rises to the surface surrounded by bubbles, and is then cooked and golden brown in about 2 minutes, the temperature is right.) Drain the rings well on kitchen paper and keep hot while you fry the remainder in batches. Sprinkle the cooked rings with more salt and pepper and serve either to accompany plain grilled meat or roasts or simply as a snack.

Serves 4–6

Kidney-stuffed Onions

4 large onions, prepared   250 ml ($\frac{1}{2}$ pint) beef stock
4 lamb's kidneys   30 ml (2 tablespoons) rum
salt and pepper

Cut the top off each onion to form a lid and, using the point of a knife, hollow out the centre of each onion until a kidney will just fit inside. Chop the onion pieces from the centres and put them in a small ovenproof dish, just large enough to hold the whole onions. Remove the skins from the kidneys and, using the sharp point of a knife, cut out the cores with- out cutting the kidneys in half. Put one kidney in each onion case, season them well with salt and pepper and put on the lids. Stand the kidney-stuffed onions in the dish and pour in the stock. It should come half-way up the onions. Add more stock, or water if necessary.

Cover the dish with a lid or foil and bake at 160°C(325°F)/ Gas 3 for 2–2$\frac{1}{2}$ hours. Twenty minutes before they are ready the kidneys should be soft enough to eat with a spoon), pour a little of the rum over each kidney and continue cooking.

Serves 4

Fish

Much of the fish we can buy in the autumn is available all year round, but hake and herring are seasonal additions to perennials such as cod and plaice on the fishmonger's slabs. Whelks which are large enough to be worth bothering with can be gathered on the seashore, or your fishmonger will supply them already cleaned and probably boiled as well. If your fishmonger is the kind of chap who has whelks, he's likely to have eels, too. And he *will* do all the preparation of an eel, so don't worry. You'll take home a neatly-wrapped paper parcel in your basket just as though you'd bought a bit of smoked haddock for your supper. I've included recipes for eel, smoked haddock, hake, whelks, kippers, herrings and the roe of the herring which is such a treat, cooked simply and served on toast.

Made-up fish dishes, that is those that require more than the fish being poached or baked with some seasonings, include the national favourite, fish and chips, with ingredients to make the right kind of chip-shop batter. It's worth noting that chip shops used to fry almost exclusively in lard, which gives a different flavour from the oil used extensively nowadays. Lard also has the advantage of setting in the chip pan and not requiring sieving and decanting after every frying session. If you're sceptical about the difference lard makes, try it just once.

Kedgeree

225 g (8 oz) long-grain rice	100 g (4 oz) butter
salt	pepper
450 g (1 lb) smoked haddock	2 large eggs, hard-boiled
	5 ml (1 level teaspoon) parsley, chopped

Sprinkle the rice into a large pan of fast-boiling salted water, stir it and cook it for 12 minutes or until tender but not squashy. Put the haddock in a pan, just cover it with cold water, and simmer for 10 minutes or until the flesh flakes easily. Drain and flake, removing skin and bones. Drain the rice very well.

Melt the butter in a large pan, add the rice and fish and stir them round together, seasoning the mixture with salt and pepper. Cut 4 slices from the middle of the eggs and chop the remainder. Stir the chopped egg into the pan with the parsley and turn at once on to a hot plate. Garnish with the egg slices.

Serves 4

Smoked Haddock Quiche

Shortcrust pastry:
150 g (6 oz) plain flour
salt
40 g (1½ oz) margarine
40 g (1½ oz) lard

1 small onion, roughly
  chopped

15 ml (1 tablespoon) oil
150 g (6 oz) smoked
  haddock, cooked
2 large eggs
125 ml (¼ pint) milk
125 ml (¼ pint) double
  cream
salt and pepper

Sift the flour and a pinch of salt into a bowl and rub in the margarine and lard. Mix to a stiff dough with cold water and roll out on a lightly-floured board. Use to line a 20-cm (8-in) flan dish, tin or flan ring standing on a baking tray. Trim the edge.

Fry the onion in the oil for 5 minutes or until it is soft but not coloured. Sprinkle over the base of the flan. Flake the cooked fish into large pieces, removing skin and bones, and cover the onion with it. Beat the eggs into the milk and cream, and season well with salt and pepper. Pour this mixture over the haddock. Bake the quiche at 220°C(425°F)/ Gas 7 for about 30 minutes, pouring any left-over egg mixture into the flan when it has cooked for about 7 minutes. Serve warm.

Serves 6

Omelette Arnold Bennett

100 g (4 oz) smoked
  haddock
50 g (2 oz) butter
125 ml (¼ pint) double
  cream

4 large eggs, separated
salt and pepper
25 g (1 oz) Parmesan
  cheese, grated

Put the smoked haddock in a small pan, just cover it with

water and bring to the boil. Cover the pan, turn off the heat and leave the haddock for 10–15 minutes, then drain and flake the fish finely, removing the skin. Heat 25 g (1 oz) butter in a small pan with 30 ml (2 tablespoons) of the cream and add the fish. Stir over a high heat for 2 minutes, then leave it to cool. Whisk the egg yolks with 15 ml (1 table-spoon) cream and salt and pepper. Whisk the egg whites stiffly and fold them into the yolks with the haddock and half the cheese. Heat the rest of the butter in a small omelette pan, add the fish mixture and cook it until the bottom is golden brown. Slide the omelette gently on to a fireproof plate, without folding it, sprinkle the top with the rest of the cheese and pour on the remaining cream. Brown the top under a hot grill and serve at once.

Serves 2

Foiled Hake

4 hake cutlets	5 ml (1 teaspoon) lemon
salt and pepper	juice, strained
	few sprigs of parsley

Butter a large piece of foil, rinse the cutlets and arrange them in one layer on the foil. Season with salt and pepper and pour on the lemon juice. Add the sprigs of parsley and wrap the foil in a parcel, double-pleating it to keep in all the flavour. Place the parcel on a baking tray and bake it at 180°C(350°F)/Gas 4 for about 20 minutes or until the fish is tender. Unwrap and arrange the steaks on hot plates and serve with plain boiled potatoes.

Serves 4

Hake with Pineapple Cream Sauce

4 medium-sized hake fillets

Cream sauce:
25 g (1 oz) butter
25 g (1 oz) plain flour
125 ml (¼ pint) milk
125 ml (¼ pint) single cream
salt and pepper

75 g (3 oz) pineapple titbits, well drained
5 ml (1 teaspoon) lemon juice, strained

Rinse the hake fillets and wrap them in a piece of buttered foil, adding 30 ml (2 tablespoons) cold water. Bake them at 180°C(350°F)/Gas 4 for about 20 minutes or until they are tender.

Meanwhile, melt the butter in a pan, stir in the flour and cook the mixture for 1 minute. Remove from the heat and gradually stir in the milk and cream. Return the pan to the heat and bring to the boil, stirring all the time, then cook the sauce for 2 minutes. Season it well with salt and pepper. Remove the fish from the oven and transfer it to a hot serving dish. Stir the pineapple pieces and lemon juice into the sauce, taste for seasoning and pour it over the fish.

Serves 4

Spanish-style Hake

75 ml (5 tablespoons) oil
1 small onion, finely chopped
3 large tomatoes, skinned
1 large potato, peeled
salt and pepper
450 g (1 lb) hake fillets
20 ml (2 dessertspoons) lemon juice, strained

15 g (½ oz) fresh white breadcrumbs
15 ml (1 level tablespoon) parsley, chopped
1 clove garlic, finely chopped

Heat 20 ml (2 dessertspoons) of the oil in a frying pan and fry the onion for 5 minutes, stirring, until it is golden brown. Chop the tomatoes, add them to the pan and continue cooking for another 15 minutes until thick, mashing the tomatoes down with a wooden spoon as they cook.

Brush 15 ml (1 tablespoon) of the oil round an ovenproof dish. Slice the potato thinly and arrange the slices in the dish. Sprinkle with salt and pepper and arrange the hake fillets on top. Pour on the lemon juice and sprinkle with salt and pepper again. Pour on 20 ml (2 dessertspoons) of the oil and 90 ml (6 tablespoons) cold water. Season the tomato mixture and spread it over the fish. Mix the breadcrumbs and parsley with the garlic and sprinkle this over the tomato sauce. Pour on the remaining oil. Bake the fish at 180°C (350°F)/Gas 4 for 30–35 minutes until the potatoes and fish are tender.

Serves 4

Jugged Kippers

4 small kippers
boiling water
1 large lemon, sliced

60 ml (4 level tablespoons)
horseradish sauce

Put the kippers in a large jug, one that will hold them covered up to their tails with water. Pour on the freshly boiling water and cover the jug with a small plate. Leave for 5 minutes, then remove and drain. Put on to 4 warm plates. Add 2 or 3 lemon slices to each plate and a spoonful of horseradish sauce.

Serves 4

Marinated Kippers

8 small kippers
1 large onion, sliced
1 bay leaf
1 large lemon
45 ml (3 tablespoons) white
　wine vinegar

60 ml (4 tablespoons)
　sunflower oil
salt and pepper

Remove the kipper fillets from the bones and make sure
there are no small bones still attached to the fillets. Arrange
them in one or two layers in a shallow dish and cover with
the onion slices separated into rings. Add the bay leaf. Cut
the lemon into wedges and squeeze the juice from one
wedge. Pour it on to the kippers. Whisk the vinegar and oil
with plenty of salt and pepper and pour this over the kipper
fillets. Cover with foil, put in the fridge and leave to marinate
for 24 hours. Serve the kipper fillets, well-drained, on small
plates with a little salad and brown bread and butter.
Garnish with the remaining lemon wedges.

Serves 4–8

Kipper Creams

450 g (1 lb) kipper fillets
¼ small onion, finely
　chopped
100 g (4 oz) butter

1 large lemon
125 ml (¼ pint) double
　cream
salt and pepper

Poach the kipper fillets in a little cold water over a gentle
heat for about 5 minutes. Fry the onion in 25 g (1 oz) of
the butter until it is soft but not coloured. Finely grate the
lemon rind and squeeze out and strain the juice. Drain the
kipper fillets, reserving the liquid, and cut them into small
pieces, removing skin and bones. Pound the fish in a bowl
with a wooden spoon, adding the lemon rind and juice and

a little of the kipper liquid to make a smooth creamy mixture. Beat in the cream and salt and pepper, tasting for seasoning before dividing the mixture between 6 small dishes. Smooth the tops and put in the fridge for 2 hours to chill. Melt the remaining butter and pour a little of it over each cream. Leave in the fridge for at least another 30 minutes to set the butter.

Serves 6

Oatmeal Herrings

4 medium-sized herrings, cleaned	salt
150 g (6 oz) medium oatmeal	25 g (1 oz) dripping

Ask your fishmonger to cut off the herring heads when he cleans the fish. Rinse them and put them skin side up on a

board. Press down with your thumb all along the backbone, then turn the fish over and remove the backbone and as many of the small bones as possible. Rinse again and pat dry. Mix the oatmeal with a good pinch of salt and use to coat the herrings on both sides. Melt the dripping in a large frying pan and fry the fish for 2–3 minutes each side. Don't add more fat, because herrings are a fatty fish and very little extra is required to fry them. Serve with fried potatoes or brown bread and butter.

Serves 4

Rollmops

6 large herrings, cleaned
375 ml (¾ pint) cider
   vinegar
3 juniper berries (optional)
3 cloves
6 peppercorns
1 bay leaf

3 medium-sized onions
30 ml (2 level tablespoons)
   made mustard
15 ml (1 level tablespoon)
   capers
2 dill-pickled cucumbers

Remove the backbones from the herrings (see Oatmeal Herrings), then rinse and dry the fish.

Put the vinegar with 375 ml (¾ pint) cold water, the juniper berries, if you are using them, cloves, peppercorns and bay leaf into a pan. Bring to the boil, then simmer for 5 minutes and allow to cool. Skin and slice the onions. Spread 5 ml (1 level teaspoon) of the mustard over the flesh of each herring and sprinkle with a few capers and onion rings. Cut each cucumber, lengthwise, into three and put a piece on each fish. Roll from the head to the tail and secure with wooden cocktail sticks. Arrange the rolls in an oven-proof dish, sprinkle with the remaining onion rings and pour on the cider vinegar. Cover the dish with foil and cook them at 180°C(350°F)/Gas 4 for about 10 minutes. Allow to cool then put in the fridge for 2 days before serving them.

Serves 6

Orange-stuffed Herrings

4 medium-sized herrings, cleaned	50 g (2 oz) fresh white breadcrumbs
	salt and pepper
Orange stuffing:	15 ml (1 level tablespoon)
1 small onion, chopped	parsley, chopped
25 g (1 oz) butter	
1 large orange	1 small lemon, thinly sliced

Remove the backbones from the herrings (see Oatmeal Herrings) and rinse the fish.

To make the stuffing, fry the onion in the butter for 5 minutes or until it is soft but not coloured. Finely grate the orange rind, then remove the peel and pith using a sharp knife and chop the flesh roughly, saving the juice. Mix the orange rind and flesh and the breadcrumbs with the onions and add salt, pepper and parsley. Mix well, adding a little of the orange juice, and divide the stuffing between the fish, filling them and folding them over so they are herring-shaped again. Arrange them in an ovenproof dish in one layer. Cover them with lemon slices and pour on 45 ml (3 tablespoons) cold water. Cover with foil and bake the fish at 180°C(350°F)/Gas 4 for about 25 minutes or until tender. Serve with the lemon slices, but drain off the cooking liquid.

Serves 4

Jellied Eels

1 kg (2 lb) eels	sprigs of parsley
1 large onion, roughly	12 peppercorns
chopped	vinegar
1 bay leaf	

The fishmonger will kill the eel for you and, if you ask him,
cut it into slices, across, each about 5 cm (2 in) thick.

Choose a shallow ovenproof dish, just deep enough to
hold the slices with a bit of headroom. Stand the slices in the
dish and pack them together, not too tightly. Sprinkle with
the onion, bay leaf, parsley sprigs and peppercorns and pour
in enough vinegar to just cover the fish. Cover with a lid or
foil and bake them at 150°C(300°F)/Gas 2 for about $2\frac{1}{2}$
hours. The time taken will depend on how thick and how
close together the pieces are, but when cooked they will feel
tender when you pierce them with a sharp knife. Remove the
lid or foil and the bay leaf, peppercorns and parsley and
leave them for a good 12 hours to cool and jell. Turn out of
the dish and serve with brown bread and butter and some
salad.

Serves 8

Eel Pie

1 clove garlic, skinned	2 large cooking apples
450 g (1 lb) eels, prepared	vinegar
ground mace	150 g (6 oz) shortcrust
salt and pepper	pastry (see page 54)
pinch of saffron	
30 ml (2 tablespoons)	
boiling water	

This is a very old recipe but, unlike some, as right for today's
tastes as it was when the cook put all the ingredients together and served it at some manor house for dinner.

Cut the clove of garlic in half and rub it round an oval pie dish. Cut the eel into small pieces and toss each piece in a little ground mace mixed with salt and pepper. Arrange the pieces in the dish. Steep the saffron in the boiling water for 10 minutes.

Meanwhile, peel and core the apples and cut them into small pieces. Simmer them in 30 ml (2 tablespoons) water until soft enough to mash to a purée. Strain the saffron liquid and pour it over the eel. Spoon the apple purée into the dish, filling any gaps. Pour on vinegar to just cover the fish, cover the pie dish with a piece of foil and bake it slowly at 150°C(300°F)/Gas 2 for 2 hours. Allow to cool, then cover the dish with shortcrust pastry and bake the pie at 200°C(400°F)/Gas 6 for about 30 minutes or until the pastry is golden brown. Serve hot, or cold when the filling will have jelled.

Serves 4–6

Whelks

30 whelks   pepper
vinegar

If you buy whelks from the fishmonger they will probably be cooked, and certainly washed. But just in case, and especially if you gather your whelks from the seashore, put them in a large bowl of plain clean water, cover the bowl with a large plate and leave them to soak for about 12 hours, changing the water frequently. This will get rid of the sand and other bits you don't want to eat. When cleaned, steam the whelks for about 1 hour over a gentle heat or drop them into boiling water and immediately pull the pan off the heat. If they boil, they toughen. After the water has cooled, take the whelks out of their shells, removing the hard shell coverings, and transfer them to small saucers. Sprinkle with a little vinegar and pepper and serve.

Serves 2–4

Whelks with Parsley Sauce

50 to 60 whelks, cleaned

Parsley sauce:
25 g (1 oz) butter
25 g (1 oz) plain flour

250 ml (½ pint) milk
salt and pepper
15 ml (1 level tablespoon)
   parsley, chopped

Steam the whelks for 1 hour over a gentle heat. Towards the end of the cooking, melt the butter in a pan and stir in the flour. Cook for 1 minute, then remove from the heat and gradually stir in the milk. Return the pan to the heat and bring to the boil, stirring, until the sauce is thick, then simmer it for 2 minutes, stirring occasionally. Season with salt and pepper and stir in the parsley. Remove the whelks from their shells, discarding the hard shell coverings, pour on the sauce and serve with plain boiled potatoes.

Serves 4

Herring Roes on Toast

225 g (8 oz) soft herring roes   4 slices fresh toast
15 g (½ oz) plain flour   cayenne pepper
salt and pepper   1 large lemon
25 g (1 oz) butter, melted

Rinse the roes and pat them dry with kitchen paper. Mix the
flour with salt and pepper and toss the roes in this to coat
them. Arrange on a grill pan, brush with half the butter and
grill slowly for about 10 minutes, turning the roes once and
brushing with the rest of the butter. Serve on hot toast,
buttered if you like, sprinkled with cayenne pepper. Cut the
lemon into wedges and use as garnish.

Serves 4

Fish Puffs

Choux paste: 100 g (4 oz) cooked white
40 g (1½ oz) butter   fish, flaked
65 g (2½ oz) plain flour   5 ml (1 level teaspoon)
2 eggs, beaten   onion, finely chopped
                                    salt and pepper
                                    oil for deep frying

Melt the butter in 125 ml (¼ pint) water, then bring to the
boil. Remove from the heat and tip in the flour. Beat until
smooth and cool enough to stand the pan on your hand.
Beat in the eggs, then mix in the fish, onion and salt and
pepper and beat well until smooth. Heat the oil to 193°C
(380°F) or until a 2.5-cm (1-in) cube of bread will brown
in 1 minute, then take up pieces of the mixture on a small
spoon and drop 6 or 7 into the oil. Fry until they are golden
brown, then remove and drain on kitchen paper and keep
hot while you fry the rest of the mixture. Serve with tartare
sauce.

Serves 4

Fish and Chips

675 g (1½ lb) white fish
salt and pepper
5 ml (1 teaspoon) lemon
    juice, strained
25 g (1 oz) plain flour

5 ml (1 level teaspoon)
    dried yeast
250 ml (½ pint) warm water
15 ml (1 tablespoon) oil
1 large egg white, whisked

Yeast batter:
125 g (5 oz) plain flour
salt

oil for deep frying
    chips (see page 13)

Rinse the fish and cut it into 100-g (4-oz) portions. Cut off
the skin, if you like, and lay the fish on a plate. Sprinkle it
with salt and pepper and the lemon juice. Season the 25 g
(1 oz) plain flour with salt and pepper and put aside.

For the batter, sift the flour with a pinch of salt into a
bowl. Sprinkle the dried yeast on to the warm water and
leave it for 15 minutes until it is frothy on top. Make a well
in the flour and mix in the yeast liquid with the oil to make a
thick creamy batter. Dry the fish and coat it with the seasoned flour. Heat the oil to 182°C(360°F) and when it is ready,
fold the whisked egg white into the batter. Dip each piece
of fish in batter, allowing the excess to drop off before
gently lowering it into the hot oil. Fry until golden brown
and crisp and serve at once with freshly cooked chips.

Serves 6

Little Fish Pies

675 g (1½ lb) plaice fillets
15 ml (1 tablespoon) lemon
    juice, strained
salt and pepper
15 ml (1 level tablespoon)
    parsley, chopped

60 ml (4 tablespoons) white
    wine
4 large potatoes, sliced
25 g (1 oz) butter, melted

Divide the plaice fillets into 4 portions and arrange them in

4 individual ovenproof pie dishes or 1 large soufflé dish.
Sprinkle them with the lemon juice, salt and pepper and
parsley and pour on the white wine. Cover the fish with the
potato slices, overlapping them to make a pattern, and brush
them with melted butter. Bake at 200°C(400°F)/Gas 6 for
about 30 minutes or until the potato topping is golden
brown and tender.

Serves 4

Fish Bake

450 g (1 lb) white fish such
  as cod or coley
675 g (1½ lb) potatoes,
  peeled
salt
50 g (2 oz) butter
40 g (1½ oz) plain flour

125 ml (¼ pint) milk
100 g (4 oz) mushrooms,
  roughly chopped
pepper
100 g (4 oz) Cheddar
  cheese, grated

Cook the fish in a little water for about 10 minutes, then
drain, reserving the cooking liquid, and flake the fish, removing the skin and bones. Cook the potatoes in salted
water for about 20 minutes. Melt 25 g (1 oz) butter in a pan,
stir in the flour and cook for 1 minute, then remove from the
heat and stir in the milk and 125 ml (¼ pint) reserved cooking
liquid. Return the pan to the heat, bring to the boil, stirring,
and simmer for 2 minutes, stirring occasionally. Simmer the
mushrooms in 15 g (½ oz) butter for about 3 minutes.
Season the sauce with salt and pepper and stir in the fish
and mushrooms. (The sauce will be quite thick at this point
but will be thinner after baking.) Turn this mixture into a
pie dish. Drain and mash the potatoes with the remaining
butter and some salt and pepper. Beat in 25 g (1 oz) of the
cheese and spread the mixture over the fish. Sprinkle with
the remaining cheese and bake at 200°C(400°F)/Gas 6 for
about 30 minutes or until the cheese topping is golden.

Serves 4–6

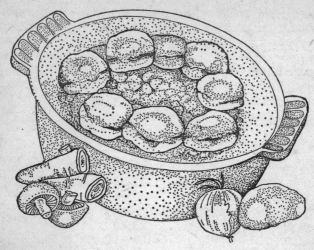

Meat

The most notable thing about the butchers' shops at this time of the year is the display of game, beginning just after 'the glorious twelfth' with grouse and followed in early September by pheasant and partridge. Game is not something the majority of us have the cash to buy, but I've included the classic methods of cooking them just in case you receive a surprise gift. Included in the recipes are details of the exact accompaniments for each bird and also how many people each one serves.

Although game is the least important meat in the cook's calendar in terms of numbers of meals, I've also given some recipes for venison, hare and rabbit and a couple for pigeons. Even though rabbit and venison are available in other seasons, the autumn months seem an appropriate time to make good use of them.

Because this is the time of year when we get out our

favourite stew and casserole pots and dishes, most of the chapter is devoted to this kind of cookery. I've given methods for preparing beef, pork, lamb, veal and chicken dishes with ideas for hearty stews and pies, plus some recipes which are more suitable for entertaining.

Steak and Kidney Pudding

450 g (1 lb) stewing steak
50 g (2 oz) ox kidney
15 g (½ oz) plain flour
salt and pepper
1 large onion, roughly
    chopped

Suet-crust pastry:
200 g (8 oz) self-raising
    flour
salt
100 g (4 oz) shredded suet

125 ml (¼ pint) good beef
    stock

Cut the steak into 2.5-cm (1-in) cubes, removing excess fat. Remove any skin and core from the kidney and cut it into small pieces. Mix the flour with a little salt and pepper and toss the meat and kidney in this to coat it. Mix with the onion.

Sift the flour and a pinch of salt for the pastry and stir in the suet. Mix to a soft but not sticky dough with cold water. Turn it on to a lightly-floured board. Cut off a quarter of the pastry for the lid and roll the large piece to a 20-cm (8-in) round. Fold it in half and, with the folded edge towards you, push the semi-circle into more of a third of a circle. Roll the point a little and you'll have a basin shape. Put your fist inside the pastry and lift it into a 1-litre (1¾-pint) pudding basin. Fill with the meat mixture and pour in the stock. Moisten the edge of the pastry in the basin. Roll the reserved pastry to a round to fit the top, put it in place and pinch the edges to seal them. Cover the pudding with a piece of greased greaseproof paper, tying it on loosely with string so the pudding has room to expand. Steam or boil it for 4 hours, pouring more boiling water into the pan as it boils away. Serve from the basin.

Serves 4

Steak and Mushroom Pie

450 g (1 lb) stewing steak
15 g ($\frac{1}{2}$ oz) plain flour
salt and pepper
125 ml ($\frac{1}{4}$ pint) good beef
   stock

100 g (4 oz) mushrooms
1 large onion, finely
   chopped
213-g (7$\frac{1}{2}$-oz) packet frozen
   puff pastry, thawed

Cut the meat into small chunks, removing excess fat. Mix the flour with a good pinch each of salt and pepper and toss the meat in this to coat it. Put the meat in an oval ovenproof pie dish and add stock. Chop the mushrooms roughly and mix with the onion into the meat. Roll the pastry on a lightly-floured board a little larger than the pie dish. Grease the rim of the dish, then cut off a 1.25-cm ($\frac{1}{2}$-in) strip from the perimeter of the pastry. Lay this band on the dish, trim and seal the ends, and moisten with a little water. Put the large piece of pastry on the pie, press the edges to seal them, then trim them. Knock up the pastry edge with the back of a knife then decorate the edge. Use any trimmings to decorate the pie, sticking them in place with a little water. Make a small hole in the centre of the pastry crust.

Bake the pie at 230°C(450°F)/Gas 8 for 15 minutes, then turn the oven down to 160°C(325°F)/Gas 3 and continue cooking for another 2–2$\frac{1}{2}$ hours, covering the pastry with a piece of greaseproof paper once it has browned enough. Test to see if the meat is cooked by pushing a skewer through the hole in the crust.

Serves 4

Beef Stroganoff

675 g (1½ lb) rump steak
25 g (1 oz) butter
1 large onion, finely
   chopped
225 g (8 oz) button
   mushrooms, sliced
salt and pepper

15 g (½ oz) plain flour
125 ml (¼ pint) good beef
   stock
142-g (5-oz) carton soured
   cream
10 ml (2 level teaspoons)
   parsley, chopped

Cut the steak into 5-cm (2-in) strips, each about 1.25-cm
(½-in) wide. Melt the butter in a frying pan and fry the onion
for 5 minutes until it is soft but not coloured. Add the steak
and cook it for 5 minutes, stirring all the time. Stir in the
mushrooms, season with salt and pepper and continue
cooking for another 5 minutes, stirring all the time until the
meat is tender. Sprinkle with the flour and mix well, then
pour in the stock and bring to the boil, stirring until the
mixture thickens. Simmer for 3 minutes, then stir in the
cream and heat gently. Garnish with the parsley and serve
with plain boiled rice.

Serves 4

Cornish Pasties

350 g (12 oz) chuck steak
3 small potatoes, peeled
1 large onion, finely
   chopped

salt and pepper
350 g (12 oz) shortcrust
   pastry (see page 54)
1 small egg, beaten

Cut the meat into 1.25-cm (½-in) dice, trimming off excess
fat. Dice the potatoes to a similar size and mix with the meat,
onion and a sprinkling of salt and pepper. Roll the pastry
on a lightly-floured board and cut it into 8 rounds, using a
saucer for size. Divide the meat mixture between the pastry
rounds and moisten the edges of the pastry. Bring the edges

together on top of the meat mixture and press them well to
seal, then crimp them between finger and thumb. Make a
hole through the sealed edge with a skewer and place the
pasties on a greased baking tray. Brush each one with egg
and bake them at 200°C(400°F)/Gas 6 for 15 minutes, then
reduce the temperature to 180°C(350°F)/Gas 4 and cook
them for another 45 minutes or until they are golden brown.
Cover the pastry with greaseproof paper if it begins to brown
too much. Test that the meat is cooked by pushing a skewer
through the hole in each one. Serve hot or cold.

Serves 8

Crown Roast of Lamb

2 pieces best end neck of
    lamb (each with 8 bones)
salt and pepper
75 g (3 oz) lard

0.5 kg (1 lb) tiny
    potatoes, prepared
0.5 kg (1 lb) peas, prepared
few sprigs of mint (optional)
16 cutlet frills

Tell your butcher that you want a crown of lamb and with
luck he'll prepare it for you. If not, bend each piece of meat
backwards in the opposite direction of the natural curve.
With the fatty sides to the inside, tie the two pieces in a
circle with the bones pointing upwards. If your butcher has
prepared it for you, he will have scraped the bones clean of
meat; if not do this with a sharp knife, exposing about
2.5 cm (1 in). Wrap a piece of foil round each bone end to
keep it white during cooking. Season the joint and spread it
with lard. Roast in the oven at 200°C(400°F)/Gas 6 for 30
minutes, then turn the oven down to 180°C(350°F)/Gas 4
and cook for a further 50 minutes or until the meat is
tender.

Thirty minutes before the joint is ready, boil the potatoes
in plenty of boiling salted water until they are tender. Boil
the peas in boiling salted water, too. Drain them both and

keep hot. Remove the joint from the oven, take off the foil covers and fill the centre of the roast with the potatoes and peas, adding a few sprigs of mint if you like. Cover each bone with a cutlet frill and serve any remaining vegetables with a knob of butter on top.

Serves 8

Lamb Cobbler

675 g (1½ lb) lean lamb	salt and pepper
25 g (1 oz) dripping	
1 large onion, roughly chopped	*Oatmeal scones:*
	100 g (4 oz) plain flour
2 large carrots, sliced	salt
125 ml (¼ pint) good stock	50 g (2 oz) medium oatmeal
30 ml (2 tablespoons) red wine (optional)	40 g (1½ oz) margarine
5 ml (1 level teaspoon) mixed dried herbs	25 g (1 oz) lard

Cut the lamb into 2.5-cm (1-in) cubes, removing excess fat and any bones. Heat the dripping in a large frying pan and fry the onion and carrots for 5 minutes, then stir in the meat pieces and fry them for 5 minutes, stirring continuously to brown them on all sides. Transfer to a deep ovenproof casserole dish and pour on the stock and wine if you are using it. Sprinkle with the herbs and salt and pepper. Cover the casserole and cook it at 160°C(325°F)/Gas 3 for 1–1½ hours or until the lamb is tender.

When it's almost ready, sift the flour and a pinch of salt for the scones and stir in the oatmeal. Rub in the margarine and lard and mix to a soft dough with cold water. Turn the dough on to a lightly-floured board and roll it to a 1.25-cm (½-in) thickness. Using a 5-cm (2-in) plain or fluted cutter, cut into rounds. Remove the casserole from the oven and take off the lid. Arrange the scones over the meat and return the casserole, uncovered, to the oven at 200°C(400°F)/Gas 6 for 35–40 minutes to cook the scones.

Serves 4–6

Tomato Bredie

8 pieces scrag or middle neck of lamb	425-g (15-oz) can tomatoes salt and pepper
1 large onion, roughly chopped	5 ml (1 level teaspoon) dried marjoram

Fry the lamb pieces in a non-stick frying pan without adding any fat. Fry them gently at first until the fat begins to run, then increase the heat and fry until the meat is brown on both sides. Remove and drain on kitchen paper. Add the onion to the pan and fry it for 5 minutes until it is soft. Put the meat in a casserole and cover with the well-drained onions. Pour on the tomatoes and their juice and break down the tomatoes with a wooden spoon. Add plenty of salt and pepper and sprinkle with the marjoram. Cover the casserole and cook it at 160°C(325°F)/Gas 3 for about 2 hours or until the meat is falling off the bones. Despite extracting some of the fat from the lamb pieces by frying, and draining the onions well, this is still a rich, cold-weather casserole with a lot of juices so serve it with plain mashed potatoes to do the mopping up.

Serves 4–6

Lancashire Hot Pot

1 kg (2 lb) best end neck of lamb	15 g ($\frac{1}{2}$ oz) plain flour salt and pepper
0.5 kg (1 lb) onions, roughly chopped	0.5 kg (1 lb) potatoes, peeled

Trim off any excess fat from the lamb and divide it into cutlets. Fry them in a non-stick pan, with the trimmed fat, very slowly at first until the fat begins to run; then increase the heat and brown them on both sides. Transfer the cutlets to a casserole dish and add the onions to the pan and fry them for 5 minutes. Sprinkle in the flour and stir it round until it browns slightly, then pour in 125 ml ($\frac{1}{4}$ pint) hot water and bring the gravy to the boil. Season it well with salt and pepper and simmer it for 3 minutes. Slice the potatoes. Pour the gravy into the casserole and arrange the slices of potato on top, overlapping them. Cover the dish. Cook the hot pot at 150°C(300°F)/Gas 2 for $2\frac{1}{2}$ hours, removing the lid for the last 30 minutes to let the potatoes brown.

Serves 6

Irish Stew

1 kg (2 lb) scrag neck of lamb
0.5 kg (1 lb) potatoes, thinly sliced
2 large onions, thinly sliced

salt and pepper
5 ml (1 level teaspoon) parsley, chopped

Cut off any excess fat from the meat. Put a layer of potato slices in a large saucepan, then add half the onion slices and all the meat. Cover with the remaining onion slices, then finally add the remaining potatoes. Be sure to season each layer as you go. Pour in 500 ml (1 pint) cold water and cover the pan with a tight lid. Bring very slowly to the boil, then keep the heat at the merest simmer and cook the stew for $2\frac{1}{2}$ hours or until the meat is tender. Serve sprinkled with the parsley.

Serves 4–6

Prune and Apricot Pork Casserole

75 g (3 oz) prunes
100 g (4 oz) dried apricots
375 ml (¾ pint) cider
1 large onion, roughly
　chopped
45 ml (3 tablespoons) oil

750 g (1½ lb) spare-rib
　chops
40 g (1½ oz) plain flour
salt and pepper
250 ml (½ pint) chicken
　stock

Rinse the prunes and apricots, put them in a bowl with the cider and leave them to soak overnight. Next day, fry the onion in the oil for 5 minutes until it is soft. Toss the chops in the flour mixed with a little salt and pepper, add them to the pan and fry them until they are brown on both sides. Transfer the meat to a casserole, leaving most of the onion in the pan. Stir in any remaining flour and cook the mixture for 1 minute, then gradually stir in the stock and the liquid from the soaked fruit. Bring to the boil, stirring all the time, and cook for 2 minutes, stirring occasionally. Season with salt and pepper. Pour this sauce over the pork, add the dried fruit and cover the casserole. Cook it at 160°C(325°F)/Gas 3 for about 2 hours or until the pork is tender.

Serves 4–6

Pork and Mushroom Roly Poly

225 g (8 oz) pork fillet
15 ml (1 tablespoon) oil
100 g (4 oz) mushrooms,
　chopped
1 small onion, finely
　chopped
5 ml (1 level teaspoon)
　lemon rind, finely grated

5 ml (1 level teaspoon)
　dried marjoram
150 g (6 oz) suet-crust
　pastry (see page 69)
tomato sauce (see page 25)

Cut the pork fillet into fine shreds and fry them gently in the hot oil, stirring all the time until tender. Mix with the mushrooms, onion, lemon rind and marjoram. Roll the pastry to a large oblong measuring about 30 by 23 cm (12 by 9 in) and spread it with the filling to within 2.5 cm (1 in) of the edges. Moisten the edges with cold water and roll up, sealing the edge. Transfer the roll to a greased baking tray with the join underneath and bake it at 200°C(400°F)/Gas 6 for about 30 minutes or until the pastry is golden and well puffed. Serve cut into thick slices with the tomato sauce.

Serves 4

Pork and Orange

4 thick pork chops
25 g (1 oz) plain flour
142-g (5-oz) carton soured
  cream
15 ml (1 tablespoon) lemon
  juice, strained

5 ml (1 level teaspoon)
  dried thyme
salt and pepper
2 large oranges, peeled

Cut off the excess fat from the pork and fry the trimmings in a pan until the fat begins to run. Dust the chops with a little flour and fry them until they are golden on both sides. Transfer them to a casserole. Mix the soured cream with the lemon juice and 60 ml (4 tablespoons) cold water. Season, and pour over the chops. Cover the dish and bake the chops at 180°C(350°F)/Gas 4 for about 45 minutes or until the chops are tender.

When they are almost ready, cut the peel and pith off the oranges using a sharp knife, then slice the flesh into rounds. Put the slices in a small pan and heat them gently, turning them over and over to make sure they heat through. Arrange them around the pork chops and serve at once.

Serves 4

Hungarian Veal Chops

4 veal chops
40 g (1½ oz) butter
15 ml (1 level tablespoon)
  paprika
salt and pepper
1 large onion, finely
  chopped

125 ml (¼ pint) white wine
125 ml (¼ pint) soured
  cream
5 ml (1 level teaspoon)
  parsley, chopped

Fry the chops in the butter until they are golden on both sides, then transfer them to a plate. Mix 5 ml (1 level teaspoon) of the paprika with a good pinch each of salt and pepper and use to dust the chops. Add the onion to the pan and fry it for 5 minutes until it is soft. Stir in the remaining paprika and cook very gently for 2 minutes. Return the chops to the pan and stir in half the wine. Put the chops and sauce in a shallow baking dish and bake them at 180°C (350°F)/Gas 4 for about 20 minutes, then keep them hot on a serving dish. Pour the remaining white wine into the baking dish and boil it hard, on top of the stove, for a few minutes to reduce it, then stir in the soured cream and simmer gently but don't let it boil. Pour over the chops and sprinkle with the parsley.

Serves 4

Osso Buco

six 5-cm (2-in) thick slices
  of shin of veal, including
  the shin bone
plain flour
75 g (3 oz) butter
125 ml (¼ pint) dry white
  wine
425-g (15-oz) can tomatoes
salt and pepper

1 clove garlic, finely
  chopped
5 ml (1 level teaspoon)
  lemon rind, finely grated
5 ml (1 level teaspoon)
  parsley, finely chopped
1 anchovy fillet, finely
  chopped

Roll the pieces of veal in flour to coat them, then fry them in the butter until they are golden brown on all sides. Pour on the wine and cook them for 15 minutes, then add the tomatoes, breaking them down with a fork, and salt and pepper. Cover and cook very slowly for 2 hours until the veal is so tender it's almost falling off the bones.

Mix the garlic, lemon rind, parsley and anchovy fillet and sprinkle this mixture over the meat a couple of minutes before you serve the dish. Turn the meat over once or twice to mix it well. Be gentle, otherwise you will separate the marrow from the bones.

Serves 4–6

Chicken in Red Wine

75 g (3 oz) streaky bacon, chopped
150 g (6 oz) mushrooms, sliced
20 very small onions, skinned or 3 large onions, sliced
25 g (1 oz) butter
10 ml (1 dessertspoon) oil
1.5-kg (3-lb) chicken
60 ml (4 tablespoons) brandy

25 g (1 oz) plain flour
375 ml (¾ pint) red wine
125 ml (¼ pint) good chicken stock
1 bay leaf
1 blade of mace
12 peppercorns
few parsley stalks
1 sprig of thyme
salt and pepper

Fry the bacon, mushrooms and onions in half the butter and oil until they are lightly browned, stirring them all the time. Remove from the pan, leaving behind the fat. Add the remaining butter and oil and the chicken to the pan and fry it on all sides until it is golden brown; this will take about 10 minutes. Pour the brandy over the chicken, heat it and light it with a match. When the flames have died down,

transfer the chicken to a deep casserole dish. Stir the flour
into the pan and cook it for 2 minutes, stirring all the time,
then add the wine and stock and boil, stirring, until the sauce
thickens. Add the bay leaf, mace, peppercorns, parsley
stalks and thyme, tied in a piece of muslin, and salt and
pepper and pour the sauce over the chicken. Add the bacon
mixture and cover the casserole. Cook at 180°C(350°F)/Gas
4 for 45 minutes or until the chicken is tender. Before you
serve it, remove the muslin bag.

Serves 6–8

Chicken Plate Pie

450 g (1 lb) cooked chicken
salt and pepper
1 large onion, roughly
  chopped
25 g (1 oz) butter

125 ml (¼ pint) chicken
  stock
250 g (10 oz) shortcrust
  pastry (see page 54)

Pull the chicken off the bones. This is best done in large
pieces, but if you are stripping a carcass and most of the
pieces are small, don't worry; although it won't look as good
when you cut into the pie, it will still taste marvellous.
Season the chicken with salt and pepper. Fry the onion in the
butter for 5 minutes until it is soft, then drain it well. Make
the chicken stock by boiling the chicken bones for 1 hour,
then let it cool; if you already have some stock, boil it down
until it is reduced to 125 ml (¼ pint) to make sure it jells when
cold.

Roll the pastry on a lightly-floured board and use half of
it to line a 23-cm (9-in) pie dish. Layer the chicken pieces
on the pastry with the onion. If some of your chicken pieces
are larger than others, use them in one layer in the middle
of the layers of the smaller chicken bits and the onion. Pour
on the cold stock. Roll the remaining pastry to a large
round. Moisten the pastry edge on the pie plate and cover

with the large round. Press the edges to seal, then trim and decorate them. Make a hole in the centre of the top crust and use the trimmings to make decorations, sticking them on with a little water. Bake the pie at 200°C(400°F)/Gas 6 for 30–35 minutes or until the pastry is golden brown. Eat cold for preference, when the stock has jellied and the pie will cut into good wedges.

Serves 6–8

Durham Pot Pie

4 large rabbit joints
50 g (2 oz) dripping
3 large carrots, sliced

3 large onions, sliced
salt and pepper
200 g (8 oz) suet-crust pastry (see page 69)

Cut the rabbit joints into small pieces and fry them in the dripping until browned on all sides. Mix with the carrots and onions and season well. Roll the pastry on a lightly-floured board until it is 5 cm (2 in) larger than the top of a 1.5-litre (2½-pint) pudding basin. Grease a 5-cm (2-in) border round the top inside edge of the basin. Cut off a 5-cm (2-in) strip of pastry from the perimeter and press this band inside the pudding basin at the top. Trim the edges and join with a little water. Moisten the top edge and put the rabbit mixture into the basin. Add 125 ml (¼ pint) cold water. Cover with the round of pastry, pinching the edges to seal. Cover with a piece of greased greaseproof paper and tie it on loosely to allow the pastry to puff up. Boil or steam it for 3½ hours, adding more boiling water to the pan as it evaporates.

Serves 4

Roman Rabbit

4 rabbit joints	25 g (1 oz) butter
salt and pepper	25 g (1 oz) plain flour
225 g (½ lb) onions, sliced	125 ml (¼ pint) milk
225 g (½ lb) carrots, sliced	100 g (4 oz) Cheddar
125 ml (¼ pint) chicken	cheese, grated
stock	

Put the rabbit joints in a pan, cover them with cold water and bring to the boil. Drain, then season the rabbit and put the joints in a casserole with the onions and carrots. Pour on the stock, cover the dish and cook it at 180°C(350°F)/Gas 4 for about 1 hour or until the rabbit is tender. Strain and reserve the stock from the casserole.

Melt the butter in a small pan, stir in the flour and cook the mixture for 1 minute. Remove from the heat and gradually stir in the rabbit stock and the milk. Return the pan to the heat, bring to the boil, stirring all the time, and cook gently for 2 minutes. Season well and stir in 75 g (3 oz) cheese. Pour the sauce over the rabbit, sprinkle the top with the remaining cheese and return the casserole to the oven for a further hour.

Serves 4

Salmi of Pigeon

6 small fat young pigeons	30 ml (2 tablespoons) oil
2 sprigs of sage	10 ml (2 level teaspoons)
3 sprigs of parsley	lemon rind, finely grated
6 large anchovy fillets	250 ml (½ pint) dry red
2 cloves garlic, crushed	wine
15 ml (1 level tablespoon)	salt and pepper
capers	

Cut all the flesh from the bones of the pigeons, keeping the breast meat as intact as possible. Cut the rest of the flesh into even-sized small pieces. Mix the giblets with the sage, parsley, anchovy fillets, garlic and capers and chop all together finely. Heat the oil in a large pan, add the pigeon breasts and the lemon rind and cook them gently until the meat has browned on both sides. Pour in the wine and bring it to the boil, then stir in the rest of the meat and the chopped giblets and season well with salt and pepper. Cover the pan with a large piece of greaseproof paper and then the lid, so that the paper forms a really good seal. Cook for 1 hour, gently, without removing the lid. This dish is best if cooked the day before you want it, cooled overnight in the fridge, and then reheated. Serve with rice.

Serves 6

Pigeon Pie

450 g (1 lb) stewing beef
2 fat young pigeons
1 large onion, finely
    chopped
45 ml (3 tablespoons) oil
12 whole tiny onions,
    skinned
100 g (4 oz) button
    mushrooms

25 g (1 oz) plain flour
250 ml (½ pint) beef stock
125 ml (¼ pint) beer
5 ml (1 level teaspoon)
    dried thyme
1 bay leaf
213-g (7½-oz) packet frozen
    puff pastry, thawed

Cut the beef into 2.5-cm (1-in) cubes. Cut the pigeons in half, removing the backbones. Fry the chopped onion in the oil for 5 minutes, then add the meat and pigeon pieces and fry them until browned on all sides. Transfer the meat to a large oval pie dish, add the whole onions and mushrooms. Stir the flour into the remaining fat in the pan and cook it for 1 minute. Remove from the heat and stir in the beef stock and beer and bring to the boil, stirring all the time. When thick, add the thyme and bay leaf and pour into the pie dish. Cover with a large piece of foil and cook at 160°C(325°F)/Gas 3 for 2½ hours or until the meat is tender. Allow to cool completely, then take off any fat.

Roll the pastry on a lightly-floured board until it is slightly larger than the pie dish. Grease the rim of the dish. Cut off a 1.25-cm (½-in) strip of pastry from the perimeter and press this on the rim, then trim and join the edges. Moisten with a little water, lift on the large piece of pastry and press the edges to seal. Trim, knock them up and decorate. Use any trimmings to decorate the top of the pie, sticking them in place with a little water. Make a hole in the top crust. Bake the pie at 230°C(450°F)/Gas 8 for 15 minutes, then lower the heat to 200°C(400°F)/Gas 6 and cook for another 15–20 minutes or until the pastry is golden and well risen.

Serves 4–6

Roast Venison

1.5-kg (3-lb) joint of venison, saddle or fillet	3 parsley stalks
2 carrots, thinly sliced	12 peppercorns, crushed
1 large onion, roughly chopped	5 ml (1 level teaspoon) salt
1 bay leaf	125 ml (¼ pint) oil
1 clove garlic, crushed	375 ml (¾ pint) red wine
	dripping
	plain flour

Put the joint of venison in a bowl. Mix together the carrots, onion, bay leaf, garlic, parsley stalks, peppercorns, salt, oil and wine, pour it over the venison and leave to marinate for 24 hours, turning the joint three or four times. Next day, remove it from the marinade and dry it thoroughly. Spread it thickly with dripping and wrap the whole joint first in greaseproof paper and then in foil. Stand the joint in a roasting tin and roast it at 180°C(350°F)/Gas 4 for 20 minutes for every 450 g (1 lb). Half an hour before the joint is ready for serving, remove the coverings, dredge the meat with flour and increase the heat to 200°C(400°F)/Gas 6. Baste the joint well and finish cooking. Serve with red-currant jelly or cranberry sauce and a gravy made from the drippings in the tin.

Serves 8

Roast Grouse

1 young grouse
salt and pepper
2 rashers streaky bacon
25 g (1 oz) butter
1 slice of toast
watercress, prepared

Fried breadcrumbs:
50 g (2 oz) fresh white
    breadcrumbs
25 g (1 oz) butter

Season the trussed bird inside and out with salt and pepper and lay the rashers of bacon over the breast. Put 25 g (1 oz) butter inside and stand the bird on the toast in a roasting tin. Roast it at 200°C(400°F)/Gas 6 for 30 minutes, removing the bacon after 20 minutes' cooking, dusting the bird with a little flour and basting it well.

Transfer it, still on the toast, to a hot serving dish and keep hot. Pour 125 ml (¼ pint) water into the roasting tin and stir it round, scraping at the bits on the tin. Bring to the boil and boil for 3 minutes, then carefully remove all grease

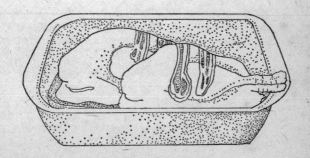

from the surface with a metal spoon. Season the gravy and
strain it into a jug. Garnish the bird with the watercress
after removing the trussing strings. Quickly fry the breadcrumbs in the butter, stirring them all the time until they
are golden brown, and serve with the grouse.

Serves 2

Roast Pheasant

1 cock pheasant
6 rashers streaky bacon
50 g (2 oz) butter
plain flour
watercress, prepared

fried breadcrumbs (see
  page 85)
thin gravy (see Roast
  Grouse)
game chips (see page 14)

Put the pheasant in a roasting tin and cover the breast with

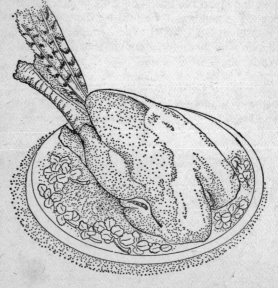

the pieces of bacon. Add the butter and roast the bird at
220°C(425°F)/Gas 7 for 20 minutes for each 450 g (1 lb) –
usually about 1 hour – basting it frequently with the butter.
About 15 minutes before the cooking time is complete,
remove the bacon and dust the breast with flour, baste well
and finish cooking. Remove the trussing strings and place
the pheasant on a hot dish garnished with the watercress.
Serve with fried breadcrumbs, thin gravy and game chips.

Serves 3-4

Roast Partridge

1 young partridge per
  person
salt and pepper
15 g (½ oz) butter per bird
2 rashers streaky bacon
  per bird

1 slice of toast per bird
watercress, prepared
1 large lemon, quartered
thin gravy (see Roast
  Grouse)
game chips (see page 14)

Season the partridge inside and out with salt and pepper.
Return the rinsed liver to the inside with the butter. Cover
the breast with the bacon rashers and put the bird on a slice
of toast. Stand it in a roasting tin and roast it at 230°C
(450°F)/Gas 8 for 10 minutes, then reduce the heat to 200°C
(400°F)/Gas 6 and continue roasting for another 15 minutes
or until the bird is well done. Serve it on its slice of toast,
after removing the trussing strings, garnished with watercress
and lemon quarters. Like grouse and pheasant, partridge is
usually accompanied by game chips, thin gravy and a tossed
green salad.

Jugged Hare

1 hare
50 g (2 oz) streaky bacon, chopped
50 g (2 oz) butter
1 large onion, roughly chopped
2 large carrots, roughly chopped
2 sticks of celery, sliced
salt and pepper

few parsley stalks
1 blade of mace
1 sprig of thyme
12 peppercorns
10 ml (2 level teaspoons) lemon rind, grated
1 litre (1¾ pints) stock
25 g (1 oz) cornflour
60 ml (4 tablespoons) port

Order the hare already jointed and ask for the blood with your order. Fry the bacon in a large frying pan until the fat begins to run, then add the butter and the hare joints, turning them until they are brown all over. Cook the hare in the frying pan if you have a good lid for it, or transfer it to a heavy saucepan. Add the onion, carrots and celery and season with salt and pepper. Tie the parsley stalks, mace, thyme and peppercorns in a small piece of muslin and add to the pan with the lemon rind. Pour on the stock (game stock preferably, but a rich beef stock will do instead), adding enough to just cover the hare. Bring to the boil, cover the pan and simmer for 3 hours or until the hare is very tender. Mix the cornflour to a smooth paste with a little water and stir it into the pan. Bring to the boil, stirring, then simmer for another 3–4 minutes. Mix together the port and blood and stir it into the pan. Reheat but do not let it boil and serve at once.

Serves 6

Rice

While half the world relies on potatoes for their main ingredient, the rest cook and eat rice for almost every meal and so for this chapter I've been able to include recipes from many parts of the globe. Some, like pilaf and risotto, will be familiar to you in one form or another but there are good sweet and savoury dishes from places like Belgium and Italy, cakes from Italy and a cold soup from Poland which show the versatility of this grain.

Everyone seems to have problems cooking rice as a vegetable accompaniment. How difficult it seems to cook it perfectly, white and fluffy with every grain separate – and how easy it is actually to achieve the desired result. It's interesting to know that you can save fuel and cook rice in the oven with your casserole and for this the one-two method is the most successful. Rice absorbs twice its volume of water and it's this fact that makes a simple recipe. It's also useful to know that you can vary the liquid in which you cook your rice – try stock or tomato juice – and that additions of herbs, cheese or other vegetables can be very successful.

Perfect Boiled Rice

40–50 g (1½–2 oz) long-grain rice per person	5 ml (1 level teaspoon) salt
	15 g (½ oz) butter

Bring a large pan of water to the boil (500 ml (1 pint) for each 50 g (2 oz) rice). Add the salt and sprinkle in the rice. Stir once to make sure the rice isn't sticking to the bottom of the pan, then boil it quickly, uncovered, for 12–15 minutes or until the rice is just soft. To test, press a grain between your finger and thumb; when it's ready it should have a slight resistance to the pressure. If it completely squashes, remember to boil for a couple of minutes less next time. The difference in time given is for varying kinds of rice. All seem to take slightly different times and the only sure test is the pinch method. As soon as the rice is cooked, drain it in a large sieve and run hot water through the grains. Allow to drain thoroughly and serve at once; if you need to keep it hot return it to the pan with the knob of butter, cover the pan with a tea towel, and leave the rice to dry out over a very low heat, stirring it once or twice with a fork to make sure it isn't catching on the bottom. Or you can spread the drained rice on a Swiss roll tin, cover it with a tea towel and put it in the oven at 150°C(300°F)/Gas 2 and leave it to dry. A low temperature should be used if you want to keep the rice hot for some length of time, although for the sake of economy, it's perhaps best to let it cool and reheat it later by steaming it for 20–25 minutes.

Oven-cooked Rice

1 cup long-grain rice	5 ml (1 level teaspoon) salt

Put the measured rice into an ovenproof dish. Pour 2 cups of water into a pan and bring to the boil with the salt, then pour this over the rice and stir well. Cover the dish tightly with a lid or foil so that no steam can escape and cook in a preheated oven – 180°C(350°F)/Gas 4 for 35–40 minutes or until the grains are just soft and all the liquid has been absorbed by the rice.

Serves 4

One-two Boiled Rice

1 cup long-grain rice   5 ml (1 level teaspoon) salt

Put the rice, with 2 cups of cold water, in a pan. Add the salt and bring quickly to the boil. Stir well and cover with a tight-fitting lid so that no steam can escape. Reduce the heat and simmer gently for 14–15 minutes. Remove from the heat and lightly fork through the rice to separate the grains. It's important not to lift the lid while the rice is cooking, because the steam will escape and the cooking time will be lengthened. Nor should you stir the rice while it simmers because the grains may break up and become soggy. And don't be tempted to increase the amount of water or you'll have a soggy mess.

Serves 4

If you serve rice often, vary it from time to time in one of the following ways:
Stock-cooked rice
Replace the water with either chicken or beef stock.
Tomato rice
Replace the water with tomato juice, either undiluted or 1 cup juice and 1 cup water.
Savoury rice
Fry 1 small chopped onion, $\frac{1}{2}$ small chopped green pepper,

2 sticks chopped celery or 2 rashers chopped streaky bacon in a little fat before you add the rice and water. Or use a combination of any of the above ingredients.

Herb rice

Add a pinch of dried herbs to the cooking liquid. Good flavours to try are sage, thyme, mixed herbs, marjoram or basil.

Curry rice

Add 5 ml (1 level teaspoon) curry powder to the cooking liquid.

Australian rice

When the rice is cooked, stir in any one of the following, or a combination: pineapple titbits, toasted flaked almonds, chopped fresh herbs, chopped canned red peppers, chopped canned apricots, sultanas, currants or seedless or stoned raisins.

Cheesy rice

When the rice is cooked, stir in finely grated Cheddar cheese.

Mushroom Risotto

100 g (4 oz) butter
1 small onion, thinly sliced
350 g (12 oz) open-cap mushrooms, thinly sliced
125 ml (¼ pint) dry white wine
0.5 kg (1 lb) Italian risotto rice
1.5 litres (2½ pints) beef stock
75 g (3 oz) Parmesan cheese, grated

Heat 50 g (2 oz) butter in a heavy pan and fry the onion for 5 minutes until it is soft but not brown. Add the mushrooms and stir to coat them well. Pour in the wine and continue cooking until the wine has almost evaporated. If this seems extravagant you can omit it, but don't substitute water for the wine. Add the rice and continue to fry until it browns slightly, then add the stock 125 ml (¼ pint) at a time and continue cooking, allowing the rice to absorb one measure of stock before you add the next one. At the end of 20 minutes' cooking, the rice will be moist, separate and tender. Stir in the rest of the butter and the cheese, then cover the pan and remove the risotto from the heat. Allow to stand for a couple of minutes before serving. Serve, if liked, with more grated Parmesan cheese.

Serves 6–8

Fried Risotto

50 g (2 oz) butter   Parmesan cheese, grated
450 g (1 lb) cooked risotto

This is an excellent way of using up any left-over rice, whether it is a cooked risotto or just a plain boiled or oven-cooked rice.

Heat the butter in a large frying pan and when it is hot add the rice, forming it into a large flat cake with a knife. Fry it over a gentle heat until the bottom forms a golden brown crust, but keep shaking the pan from time to time to make sure it isn't sticking and burning. Put a plate over the rice and invert the pan so the rice is on the plate, cooked side upwards. Now slide the rice cake back into the pan to cook the other side until it, too, is golden brown. Cut the rice into wedges and serve with the cheese.

Serves 4

Savoury Rice Ring

0.5 kg (1 lb) long-grain   1 small green pepper,
    cold cooked rice   chopped
60 ml (4 level tablespoons)   6 radishes, chopped
    mayonnaise   salt and pepper
¼ cucumber, chopped   watercress, prepared

Mix the cooked rice with the mayonnaise and the chopped vegetables and season well with salt and pepper. Pack the rice into a 1.75-litre (3-pint) ring mould and smooth the surface, then put it in the fridge for 4 hours to chill and set. Turn out the ring on to a serving dish by inverting the ring on to a plate and leaving the rice to drop out on its own. Fill the centre with watercress and serve the rice ring with other salads, cold meat, roast chicken or pork.

Serves 6–8

Cold Cherry and Rice Soup

425-g (15-oz) can stoned cherries
25 g (1 oz) long-grain rice

142-g (5-oz) carton soured cream

Drain the cherries, reserving the juice. Make it up to 1.5 litres (2½ pints) with cold water. Bring to the boil, sprinkle in the rice and simmer it for 30 minutes or until the rice is tender. Five minutes before the end of the cooking time, add the cherries to the pan. Allow to cool, then chill in the fridge. Serve in wide dishes with a good dollop of soured cream on each one.

Serves 4

Chinese Fried Vegetable Rice

4 large eggs, beaten
5 ml (1 level teaspoon) salt
100 g (4 oz) frozen peas
100 g (4 oz) button mushrooms
50 g (2 oz) butter
30 ml (2 tablespoons) condensed beef stock

15 ml (1 tablespoon) soy sauce
60 ml (4 tablespoons) corn oil
1 large onion, finely chopped
225 g (8 oz) long-grain cold cooked rice

Mix the beaten eggs with the salt. Put the peas and mushrooms in a small pan with the butter, condensed beef stock and soy sauce and stir over a moderate heat until the peas are almost cooked. Heat the oil in a large pan and when very hot stir-fry the onion for 1 minute. Pour on the beaten egg and tilt the pan so that the egg will cover the base of the pan. Lower the heat and scramble the egg and onion. Add the rice, and scramble thoroughly with the egg. Pour on the peas and mushrooms. Continue to stir until the rice is hot, then serve at once.

If you wish you can add some meat to this dish. Dice 50–75 g (2–3 oz) very finely and fry it quickly, stirring all the time, in 15 ml (1 tablespoon) oil. Add the peas and mushrooms with the butter, stock and sauce to this pan and finish the rice as described.

Serves 4–6

Kheema Biryani

pinch of saffron
30 ml (2 tablespoons)
  boiling water
225 g (8 oz) long-grain
  rice
salt
125 ml (5 oz) butter,
  melted
1 small onion, finely
  chopped
5 ml (1 level teaspoon)
  ground cumin

5 ml (1 level teaspoon)
  ground turmeric
3 ml ($\frac{1}{2}$ level teaspoon)
  ground coriander
5 ml (1 level teaspoon)
  ground cardamom
0.5 kg (1 lb) lean raw lamb,
  minced
1 large egg, hard-boiled

Put the saffron into a cup, pour on the boiling water and leave to soak. Rinse the rice 3 or 4 times in a sieve to remove the excess starch. Continue rinsing until the water runs clear. Bring 375 ml ($\frac{3}{4}$ pint) cold water to the boil in a saucepan. Add 5 ml (1 level teaspoon) salt and sprinkle in the rice. Boil hard, stirring occasionally, for about 8 minutes, then strain into a sieve and put on one side.

Heat 45 ml (3 tablespoons) of the melted butter in a large frying pan and when it is really hot, add the onion and a pinch of salt. Fry for about 5 minutes or until the onion is soft. Add the ground cumin, turmeric, coriander and cardamom, stir well, then add the minced lamb and fry it for about 10 minutes, stirring all the time.

Heat the remaining melted butter in a pan or casserole that can be put into the oven later on. Add the cooked rice and stir it well to coat every grain with butter. Remove from the heat and take out about a third of the rice. Spread the remainder evenly over the base of the pan or casserole. Pour in about half the saffron and the soaking liquid. Add half the lamb mixture. Spread with half the remaining rice, add the rest of the lamb and top with the last of the rice. Pour the remaining saffron, in a dribble, evenly over the top. Pour in 250 ml ($\frac{1}{2}$ pint) cold water, or preferably some lamb

stock made by boiling lamb bones, down the side of the dish.
Bring to the boil quickly, then cover the pan or casserole
first with a piece of foil and then a lid and bake it at 180°C
(350°F)/Gas 4 for about 25 minutes until the rice is tender
and has absorbed all the liquid. Remove the lid and foil,
fluff up the rice with a fork and serve garnished with slices
of hard-boiled egg.

Serves 6

Rice Pudding

40 g (1½ oz) short-grain   500 ml (1 pint) milk
   rice, rinsed   15 g (½ oz) butter
25 g (1 oz) granulated sugar   ground nutmeg

Put the rice in a greased ovenproof dish with the sugar.
Pour on the milk, then cut the butter into fine pieces and
sprinkle into the pudding. Sprinkle with nutmeg and bake
at 150°C(300°F)/Gas 2 for 2 hours, stirring the pudding after
30 minutes.

Serves 4

Toffee Rice

40 g (1½ oz) short-grain rice   75 g (3 oz) brown sugar
500 ml (1 pint) milk

Rinse the rice and put it in a greased ovenproof and flame-
proof dish. Pour on the milk and stir well. Bake at 150°C
(300°F)/Gas 2 for 2 hours, stirring the pudding after 30
minutes. Remove from the oven and sprinkle the sugar
all over the surface. Put it under a very hot grill, watching it
and turning it when necessary, until the topping has melted
and turned to a rich golden caramel.

Serves 4–6

Fruity Rice Pudding

50 g (2 oz) sultanas
2 large cooking apples,
  sliced
25 g (1 oz) dried apricots
40 g (1½ oz) short-grain
  rice, rinsed

500 ml (1 pint) milk
25 g (1 oz) granulated sugar
2 large eggs, separated
100 g (4 oz) caster sugar

Put the sultanas, apple slices and apricots in a pan with 125 ml (¼ pint) cold water and simmer them for 10 minutes until the apples have cooked but are still whole. Stir to mix well. Put the rice with the milk in a heavy saucepan and simmer them together for about 40 minutes until the rice is creamy and thick. Stir in the granulated sugar and egg yolks. Spoon the fruit mixture into an ovenproof pie dish and cover with the rice. Whisk the egg whites until they are stiff, then fold in the caster sugar. Cover the rice with meringue and put the pudding in the oven at 220°C(425°F)/ Gas 7 for 5–10 minutes or until the meringue peaks are golden.

Serves 6–8

Pear Condé

50 g (2 oz) short-grain rice,
  rinsed
500 ml (1 pint) milk
25 g (1 oz) granulated sugar

225 g (8 oz) pears, sliced
25 g (1 oz) caster sugar
200 g (8 oz) redcurrant jelly
juice of 1 lemon, strained

Put the rice and milk in a heavy pan with the granulated sugar and cook it for 40 minutes until it is creamy, stirring the mixture occasionally. Poach the pear slices in the caster sugar dissolved in 60 ml (4 tablespoons) cold water, until they are tender. Remove the pears and drain, leaving the liquid in the pan. Divide the rice between 4 or 6 serving dishes and top with the poached pear slices. Add the red-currant jelly to the syrup in the pan with the lemon juice and stir over a gentle heat until it is smooth and thick. Spoon over the pears and leave to cool before serving, although it is also delicious hot.

Serves 4–6

Rich Rice

500 ml (1 pint) creamed rice (see Pear Condé)
142-ml (5-oz) carton double cream
8 glacé cherries, quartered

25 g (1 oz) flaked almonds, toasted
25 g (1 oz) sultanas
5 ml (1 level teaspoon) orange rind, grated

Cook the rice and when it is ready, whisk the cream to soft peaks. Stir half the cream into the rice with the cherries, almonds and sultanas. Stir the orange rind into the remaining cream. Divide the rice between serving dishes and top with a little cream.

Serves 4–6

Ground Rice Moulds

500 ml (1 pint) milk
1 bay leaf
75 g (3 oz) ground rice
15 g ($\frac{1}{2}$ oz) caster sugar

25 g (1 oz) butter
2 large eggs, beaten
golden syrup, heated

Bring the milk to the boil with the bay leaf, turn off the heat and allow it to stand for 30 minutes. Remove the bay leaf and bring the milk back to the boil, then sprinkle on the ground rice and simmer gently, stirring occasionally, for 20 minutes. Beat in the sugar, butter and eggs and turn the mixture into 4 sponge pudding moulds. Bake them at 180°C

(350°F)/Gas 4 for about 30 minutes, then turn them out and serve with golden syrup.

Serves 4

Italian Rice Cake

650 ml (1½ pints) milk
175 g (6 oz) short-grain rice, rinsed
pinch of salt
100 g (4 oz) sugar
2 large eggs, separated
5 ml (1 level teaspoon) lemon rind, grated
25 g (1 oz) chopped mixed peel

almond essence
50 g (2 oz) flaked almonds, toasted
15 g (½ oz) fine dry breadcrumbs
30 ml (2 tablespoons) Maraschino or cherry liqueur
icing sugar

Bring the milk to the boil in a heavy saucepan, then sprinkle in the rice with the salt and 50 g (2 oz) sugar. Stir well and simmer gently until the rice is almost tender. Beat the egg yolks with the remaining sugar until the mixture is light and fluffy, then beat in the cooled rice, lemon rind, mixed peel and a few drops of almond essence. Stir in the toasted almonds. Whisk the egg whites until they are stiff, then fold them into the rice mixture. Butter a 15-cm (6-in) cake tin with a fixed base, sprinkle with the breadcrumbs to coat the base and sides, then pour in the rice mixture. Bake at 160°C(325°F)/Gas 3 for 1½–2 hours until the cake is firm with a golden top. Remove and allow to cool. Using a fine skewer, prick holes all over the surface of the cake, spoon on the Maraschino or other cherry liqueur and leave it in the tin overnight. Next day, turn it out, sprinkle it all over with icing sugar and serve.

Serves 8

Little Rice Cakes

450 g (1 lb) short-grain rice, rinsed
pinch of salt
500 ml (1 pint) milk
5 ml (1 level teaspoon) baking powder
75 g (3 oz) granulated sugar

175 g (6 oz) plain flour, sifted
oil for deep frying
25 g (1 oz) icing sugar, sifted
5 ml (1 level teaspoon) ground cinnamon

Bring a large pan of water to the boil, then add the rice and salt and cook, stirring occasionally, for 10 minutes. Drain well and return the rice to the pan, then pour in the milk and simmer slowly until the rice has absorbed all the milk. Beat in the baking powder and leave overnight. Next day, turn the mixture into a bowl and beat in the sugar and flour. Shape into small flat cakes. Heat the oil to 182°C(360°F) and cook the cakes, a few at a time, until they are golden brown. Remove and drain on kitchen paper. Sift the icing sugar with the cinnamon, sprinkle it over the cakes and serve at once.

Makes 50

Rice Cake from Liège

213-g (7½-oz) packet frozen puff pastry, thawed
750 ml (1½ pints) milk
150 g (5 oz) short-grain rice, rinsed
pinch of salt

3 ml (½ level teaspoon) ground cinnamon
175 g (6 oz) caster sugar
15 ml (1 level tablespoon) cornflour
3 large eggs, separated

Roll the pastry thinly on a lightly-floured board and use to line a 20-cm (8-in) flan dish or ring standing on a baking tray. Bring the milk to the boil, sprinkle in the rice and bring back to the boil, stirring all the time. Now add the salt, cinnamon and sugar and continue to cook over a very gentle heat for about 40 minutes, stirring occasionally, until tender. Blend the cornflour with a little cold water, stir it into the rice with the egg yolks and whisk well to mix. Continue stirring until the mixture thickens. Whisk the egg whites stiffly, allow the thickened rice to cool and fold in the egg whites. Pour this mixture, when it has cooled, into the flan and bake it at 220°C(425°F)/Gas 7 for about 30 minutes, sprinkling the surface of the cake with a little caster sugar half-way through the cooking. Serve hot sprinkled with extra sugar, or allow to cool.

Serves 8

Caramel Rice

250 ml (½ pint) milk
250 ml (½ pint) single
 cream
40 g (1½ oz) short-grain
 rice, rinsed

rind of 1 lemon, thinly
 pared
75 g (3 oz) caster sugar
6 large egg yolks

Put the milk, cream, rice and lemon rind in a pan, bring to the boil slowly and simmer gently for 40 minutes or until tender, stirring occasionally. Meanwhile, put the sugar in a heavy pan and heat it gently until it begins to melt. Continue heating the syrup until it is a rich brown. Pour the caramel into a 1.25-litre (2-pint) ovenproof basin and swirl it round to coat the sides well. Beat the egg yolks, then gradually beat in the rice mixture, removing the lemon rind. Turn this mixture into the basin and stand it in a meat tin half-full of boiling water. Bake it at 150°C(300°F)/Gas 2 for about 30 minutes until firm. Allow to cool, then chill overnight in the fridge and turn out next day on to a serving dish.

Serves 4–6

Puddings

Fruits which ripen at this time of the year are apples, pears, plums, damsons, greengages and blackberries – all of which I've used to make different kinds of puddings. Some of these are light, some are more robust for the colder days and some are here simply because they're the nicest way of preparing particular fruits.

Again, I've looked around the world for interesting recipes and have included those which use our fruits in less familiar ways. The classic Tarte Normande from France and Germany's Apfel Strudel are two good examples and although you may well know of them, you might not have tried them for yourselves. However, Chinese Toffee Apples, which you might have ordered to round off a meal in a Chinese restaurant, will be quite new to many people.

Having twice been the owner of a mulberry tree, I certainly won't move house again if I'm lucky a third time. The mulberry is a delicious fruit. It looks like a large loganberry though it is slightly more tart even when fully ripe. If you

have a mulberry tree in your garden, you probably wonder
if you can do anything with them. Certainly they never go
to waste, because the birds love them. But pick a few one
day (use rubber gloves because they're very juicy and splash
everywhere) and turn them into a pie – the recipe is here –
then later you can experiment with them, using them just
as you would use loganberries or blackberries.

Eve's Pudding

0.5 kg (1 lb) Bramley
   cooking apples
75 g (3 oz) granulated sugar
pinch of ground cloves
50 g (2 oz) butter, softened

50 g (2 oz) caster sugar
1 large egg, beaten
100 g (4 oz) self-raising
   flour, sifted
milk to mix

Peel, core and thickly slice the apples and put them in a
greased 750-ml (1½-pint) ovenproof pie dish. Sprinkle with
the sugar and ground cloves and stir to mix well. Cream the
butter and sugar until they are soft and fluffy, then beat in
the egg. Fold in the flour and mix to a soft dropping consistency with the milk. Spread quickly over the apples and
bake at 180°C(350°F)/Gas 4 for 40–45 minutes until the
topping is well-risen and golden brown. Serve hot with
custard.

Serves 4

Apple Dumplings

4 large cooking apples
213-g (7½-oz) packet frozen
   puff pastry, thawed

60 ml (4 level tablespoons)
   raspberry jam
15 g (½ oz) caster sugar

Peel and core the apples, making sure you remove every bit.
Keep the apples whole. Roll the pastry on a lightly-floured

board to a large square – large enough to cut into 4 smaller squares, each of which will be able to completely enclose an apple. When cut, put an apple, stalk end down, in the middle of each pastry square. Fill the apple centres with the jam, moisten the edges of the pastry, bring the corners to the top of the apple and pinch them well to seal. Flatten the joins if necessary to make sure the apple will stand on them. Brush the pastry with a little water and decorate if liked with two leaves for each apple cut from the pastry trimmings. Brush again lightly with cold water, sprinkle with sugar, and bake them at 200°C(400°F)/Gas 6 for 20 minutes, then lower the heat to 180°C(350°F)/Gas 4 and bake for 10–15 minutes more until the pastry is golden and flaky. Serve with cream.

Serves 4

Mulberry Pie

150 g (6 oz) shortcrust
 pastry (see page 54)
0.5 kg (1 lb) mulberries (or
 mulberries and apples
 mixed)

100 g (4 oz) granulated
 sugar

Roll the pastry thinly and use half to line a 20-cm (8-in) pie plate. Pick over the mulberries, removing the stalks. Cover the pastry with the fruit, mixed with some sliced apple if liked. Sprinkle with the sugar. Moisten the pastry edge on the plate and cover with the remaining pastry. Press the

edges to seal, trim and decorate them. Decorate the top with
the pastry trimmings, sticking them in place with a little
water. Bake at 220°C(425°F)/Gas 7 for 20 minutes, then
lower the heat to 180°C(350°F)/Gas 4 and continue cooking
for another 15–20 minutes or until the pastry is golden
brown. Sprinkle with a little sugar to serve.

Serves 6–8

Greengage Amber

100 g (4 oz) shortcrust   175 g (6 oz) caster sugar
  pastry (see page 54)   2 large eggs, separated
0.5 kg (1 lb) greengages

Use the pastry to line an 18-cm (7-in) pie dish or flan dish.
Line it with greaseproof paper, fill it with baking beans and
bake blind at 200°C(400°F)/Gas 6 for about 15 minutes,
then remove the beans and paper and return to the oven for
another 5 minutes. Remove the stalks from the greengages,
cut them in half, remove the stones and arrange the fruit in
a pan with 125 ml ($\frac{1}{4}$ pint) cold water. Simmer very gently
until the fruit is really soft and will mash to a purée. Stir in
100 g (4 oz) sugar and when it has cooled a little beat in the
egg yolks. Allow to cool completely before putting the greengage purée into the pastry case. Whisk the egg whites until
they are stiff, then whisk in half the remaining sugar. Finally
fold in the last of the sugar and pile the meringue over the
greengage purée, making sure it is covered. Return the
pudding to the oven and cook it at 150°C(300°F)/Gas 2 for
30–35 minutes or until the meringue is crisp and lightly-
coloured. Serve hot or cold.

Serves 4–6

Apple Crumble

675 g (1½ lb) cooking
  apples, thickly sliced
75 g (3 oz) butter
150 g (6 oz) plain flour,
  sifted

75 g (3 oz) caster sugar
5 ml (1 level teaspoon)
  lemon rind, finely grated

Arrange the apples in an ovenproof dish. Rub the butter into
the flour, then stir in the sugar and lemon rind. Sprinkle this
over the apples and bake at 200°C(400°F)/Gas 6 for 30–40
minutes or until the top is golden brown. Serve hot or cold
with custard or cream.

Serves 4

Cream Cheese Dumplings with Spiced Pear Sauce

350 g (12 oz) cream cheese
3 large eggs, separated
25 g (1 oz) caster sugar
25 g (1 oz) unsalted butter,
  softened
75 g (3 oz) plain flour,
  sifted

675 g (1½ lb) cooking pears
50 g (2 oz) granulated
  sugar
50 g (2 oz) butter
5 ml (1 level teaspoon)
  ground mixed spice
pinch of salt

Choose a dry cream cheese for this recipe, but if you can
only find a moist one, adjust the egg yolks, adding 2 instead
of 3. Push the cheese through a sieve, then beat in the egg
yolks, one at a time. Beat in the caster sugar and unsalted
butter, then add the flour and stir until the flour has been
incorporated. Whisk the egg whites until they are stiff but
not dry and fold them into the cheese mixture with a large
metal spoon. Roll the dough into 16 small dumplings,
stand them on a baking tray and put them in the fridge
for 30 minutes to rest.

Meanwhile, peel and core the pears and cut them into

small pieces. Put them in a pan with 250 ml ($\frac{1}{2}$ pint) cold water and simmer them until they are soft enough to make a purée. Either mash with a wooden spoon until smooth or push them through a sieve and return the mixture to the pan. Stir in the granulated sugar, butter and mixed spice and cook the purée for a few minutes until it is fairly thick.

Bring a large pan of water to the boil and add the salt. Drop in 6 to 8 dumplings at a time and stir them once or twice to prevent them sticking to each other and the pan. Then lower the heat and simmer them for 5–7 minutes until they feel firm. Lift out with a draining spoon and drain them well on kitchen paper or a tea towel. Cover them to keep them hot while you poach the remainder. Serve them on a hot plate, covered with the pear sauce.

Serves 6–8

Baked Apples

4 large cooking apples   25 g (1 oz) butter
50 g (2 oz) Demerara sugar

Wipe the apples and remove the cores. Cut through the skin around the equator of the apple. Stand them in a shallow ovenproof dish and pour in 60 ml (4 tablespoons) cold water. Fill the centres of the apples with the sugar and top with the butter. Bake at 200°C(400°F)/Gas 6 for 45 minutes to 1 hour or until the apples are soft and collapsing a little. Serve hot or cold with custard or cream.

Serves 4

Tarte Normande

100 g (4 oz) shortcrust
  pastry (see page 54)
4 large cooking apples,
  sliced
25 g (1 oz) butter
100 g (4 oz) granulated
  sugar

60 ml (4 tablespoons) white
  wine (optional)
ground cinnamon
5 ml (1 level teaspoon)
  lemon rind, grated
2 eating apples, thinly
  sliced

Roll the pastry thinly and use to line a 20-cm (8-in) flan dish.
Put it in the fridge to rest while you make the filling. Reserve the apple peels and cores. Put the apple slices with the
butter, half the sugar and the white wine (or the same amount
of cold water) with some ground cinnamon to taste into a
saucepan and simmer gently until the apples are soft enough
to purée. Push them through a sieve and if the purée is very
soft, heat it gently in an uncovered pan until it thickens.
Allow to cool completely.

Meanwhile, boil the apple peelings and cores with the rest
of the sugar, the lemon rind and 125 ml (¼ pint) cold water
until you have a thick syrup. Strain and keep on one side.
Turn the cold apple purée into the pastry case and top with
the sliced eating apples, arranging them in concentric circles.
Bake the flan at 200°C(400°F)/Gas 6 for 30–35 minutes,
covering the apples with a piece of paper if they brown too
quickly. Remove from the oven and spoon on the syrup to
cover the apples completely. Serve hot or cold.

Serves 6–8

Pears in Red Wine

100 g (4 oz) sugar lumps
125 ml (¼ pint) good red
  wine
strip of lemon rind
2.5-cm (1-in) piece of
  cinnamon stick

6 ripe dessert pears
5 ml (1 level teaspoon)
  arrowroot
25 g (1 oz) flaked almonds,
  toasted

Put the sugar in a pan with the wine, lemon rind and cinnamon stick and 125 ml (¼ pint) cold water. Heat slowly to
dissolve, then bring to the boil and boil for 1 minute. Peel
the pears carefully, keeping them whole and leaving the
stalk in place. Using the point of a sharp little knife, remove
the cores from the base, making sure every bit is cut away.
Put the peeled pears at once into the syrup, standing them
upright. It's best to choose a suitable ovenproof dish before
you start; one that will hold the pears with little extra room
is ideal. Pour on the syrup and cover the dish with a lid or a
tent of foil and poach the pears at 180°C(350°F)/Gas 4 for
30 minutes. When cooked, remove the pears and strain the
syrup back into the pan. Blend the arrowroot with a little
cold water, pour in some hot syrup and return to the pan.
Bring to the boil, stirring all the time, until the sauce thickens
and clears. Simmer for 1 minute. Arrange the pears in a
serving dish, pour on the wine sauce and sprinkle with the
almonds.

Serves 6

Plums with Almond Dumplings

250 ml (½ pint) milk
pinch of salt
25 g (1 oz) butter
100 g (4 oz) semolina
1 large egg, beaten

75 g (3 oz) caster sugar
5 ml (1 teaspoon) almond
  essence
0.5 kg (1 lb) plums
ground cinnamon

Pour the milk into a pan, add the salt and butter and heat until the milk boils. Pour in the semolina, slowly so that the milk doesn't stop boiling, stirring all the time. Cook gently, stirring, until the semolina is thick. Remove from the heat and beat in the egg, one-third of the sugar and the almond essence. When the mixture is cool enough to handle, form it into small dumplings. Bring a large pan of water to the boil and lower in the dumplings, a few at a time because they need room in which to move as they cook. Stir once or twice in the first few moments to prevent them sticking to each other or the bottom of the pan. Lower the heat and simmer them for about 15 minutes, without stirring. They are ready when they rise to the top of the water. Drain well and transfer them to a hot dish while you cook another batch.

Meanwhile, remove the plum stalks and put the plums in a pan with 125 ml (¼ pint) cold water. Bring slowly to the boil, then simmer them until they are tender but still whole. Stir in the remaining sugar and turn them into a serving dish. Transfer the dumplings on to the plums and serve at once sprinkled with a little cinnamon.

Serves 4–6

Plums in Port

75 g (3 oz) granulated sugar	0.5 kg (1 lb) plums, stoned
ground cinnamon	60 ml (4 tablespoons) port

Put the sugar with 250 ml (½ pint) cold water in a pan and heat it gently to dissolve the sugar, then bring to the boil and boil hard for 2 or 3 minutes until syrupy. Stir in ground cinnamon to taste. Add the plum halves and poach them very gently until they are tender, then pour in the port and serve hot or cold with shortbread fingers.

Serves 4–6

Apfel Strudel

50 g (2 oz) butter, melted
60 ml (4 tablespoons) tepid
water
½ large egg, beaten
4 drops white vinegar
125 g (5 oz) plain flour
pinch of salt
1 kg (2 lb) cooking apples,
thickly sliced
75 g (3 oz) caster sugar

5 ml (1 level teaspoon)
nutmeg
50 g (2 oz) sultanas
75 g (3 oz) ground almonds
5 ml (1 level teaspoon)
lemon rind, grated
50 g (2 oz) dried
breadcrumbs
25 g (1 oz) icing sugar,
sifted

Pour ¼ of the butter into a mixing bowl and stir in the water, egg and vinegar. Sift the flour and salt and mix into the liquid for at least 5 minutes until you have a firm dough. Form it into a ball and knead it on a lightly-floured surface for 10 minutes or until it is smooth and elastic. Form into a ball again, put it on a floured spot on your work surface, cover it with a warmed, not really hot, earthenware bowl and leave it for 30 minutes.

Cover the kitchen table with an old tablecloth, sprinkling it well with flour. Brush the dough with a little melted butter and roll it until it is very thin, then begin to stretch it. The easiest way is to put the backs of your hands under the dough and, starting in the centre, lift and stretch the dough towards you. When each section is thin enough to read through, work on the next one. Work quickly; it doesn't matter if the dough tears but try and mend the large holes by pinching the edges together again. Trim off the thick edge with scissors.

Mix the apples with the caster sugar, nutmeg, sultanas, ground almonds and lemon rind. Brush the dough with melted butter, sprinkle it with the breadcrumbs and place the apple filling in a thick band along the edge nearest to you to within 5 cm (2 in) of the ends. Now roll it like a Swiss roll, using the tablecloth to help you. Brush the top with the remaining melted butter and unless you have an enormous

oven and baking tray, cut the strudel in half and place it on
2 greased baking trays. Bake it at 230°C(450°F)/Gas 8 for
10 minutes, then reduce the heat to 200°C(400°F)/Gas 6 and
continue to bake for another 15–20 minutes until the strudel
is crisp and brown. Sift the icing sugar over the top and serve
cut into thick slices.

Serves 6–8

Blackberry and Apple Compôte

125 g (5 oz) granulated   450 g (1 lb) eating apples
  sugar   225 g (½ lb) blackberries

Put the sugar with 375 ml (¾ pint) cold water in a pan and
heat slowly until the sugar has dissolved, then bring to the
boil and boil hard for 2 or 3 minutes until syrupy. Meanwhile, prepare the apples. You can use cooking apples but
you do need a variety which keeps its shape. Bramleys won't
do because they quickly go to a pulp. Peel, core and thickly
slice the apples and put them immediately into the syrup to
prevent them going brown. Bring the syrup slowly to the
boil, let it boil fast, then lower the heat and simmer the fruit
very gently for 5 minutes. Pick over the blackberries, rinse
them and add them to the pan and simmer both fruits together for another 10 minutes until they are tender but still
whole. Serve hot or chilled with whipped cream.

Serves 6

Austrian Curd Cake

65 g (2½ oz) butter
125 g (5 oz) caster sugar
275 g (10 oz) smooth curd
    cheese, softened
2 large eggs, separated
50 g (2 oz) ground almonds
50 g (2 oz) sultanas

25 g (1 oz) semolina
1 large lemon

Plum sauce:
0.5 kg (1 lb) plums or
    damsons
50 g (2 oz) granulated sugar

Cream the butter until it is very soft, then beat in the sugar and curd cheese very gradually until the mixture is light and creamy. Beat in the egg yolks, one at a time, then stir in the ground almonds, sultanas and semolina. Finely grate the rind from the lemon and squeeze out and strain the juice. Stir both into the mixture. Whisk the egg whites until they are stiff but not dry and fold them quickly into the mixture. Turn it into a greased 15-cm (7-in) cake tin with a fixed base and bake it at 190°C(375°F)/Gas 5 for 45–50 minutes.

While the cake bakes, rinse the plums or damsons and put them in a large pan with 125 ml (¼ pint) cold water. Put the lid on the pan and simmer until the plums are soft. Push them through a sieve to make a purée and sweeten the purée with the granulated sugar, heating it gently in the rinsed pan. Allow both the cake and the plum sauce to cool, then serve together.

Serves 6–8

Plum and Cinnamon Pudding

125 g (5 oz) plain flour
10 ml (1 level dessertspoon)
    ground cinnamon
100 g (4 oz) golden syrup
65 g (2½ oz) butter
1 large egg, beaten

90 ml (6 tablespoons) warm
    water
5 ml (1 level teaspoon)
    bicarbonate of soda
caster sugar
plum sauce (see above)

Sift the flour and cinnamon together. Warm the golden syrup with the butter until the butter has melted but the mixture isn't too hot, then beat in the egg, water and bicarbonate of soda. Pour this mixture into the flour and beat it well for a few seconds. Pour it at once into a well-greased and greaseproof paper-lined Swiss roll tin and bake it at 180°C(350°F)/Gas 4 for 6–8 minutes or until it is firm to the touch and shrinking slightly from the edges of the tin. Turn it straight out on to a sheet of greaseproof paper heavily dredged with caster sugar. Quickly trim the edges and spread it lightly with the plum purée. Cut into squares, pile them on a serving dish, dredge again with caster or icing sugar and serve hot with cream.

Serves 6–8

Caramel Apples

175 g (6 oz) granulated
  sugar
6 Cox's eating apples,
  quartered and cored

rind of 1 orange, finely
  shredded
75 g (3 oz) lump sugar

Put the granulated sugar in a pan with 375 ml (¾ pint) cold water, dissolve the sugar over a gentle heat, then boil the syrup hard for 1 minute. Put the apple quarters into the syrup as soon as they are prepared to prevent them turning brown, cover the pan and simmer the apples for 10 minutes or until they are tender but not breaking up. Remove from the heat and leave, covered, until they are cold. Boil the orange rind shreds in a little water, then reduce the heat and simmer them for 5 minutes. Drain and refresh under running cold water. Dissolve the lump sugar slowly in 60 ml (4 tablespoons) cold water, then boil it rapidly to a rich brown colour or until the thermometer registers 149°C(300°F). Pour it into an oiled tin and let it set, then turn it on to a wooden board and crush it into fine pieces. Arrange the

apples in a serving dish, pour on the syrup then sprinkle
with the toffee pieces and the orange rind shreds. Serve with
cream.

Serves 6

Pears Mirabelle

1 medium-sized lemon
375 ml (¾ pint) milk
3 large eggs, separated
40 g (1½ oz) caster sugar
15 ml (1 level tablespoon)
  powdered gelatine
50 g (2 oz) brown
  breadcrumbs, toasted

142-g (5-oz) carton double
  cream, whipped
50 g (2 oz) granulated sugar
3 dessert pears, halved and
  cored
450 g (1 lb) red plums

Thinly pare the rind off the lemon and put it in a pan with
the milk. Bring the milk slowly to the boil, then leave it to
stand for 30 minutes. Cream the egg yolks with the caster
sugar, strain on the milk and return to a double saucepan
and stir it over a gentle heat until the mixture thickens. Don't
let it boil. Strain it into a basin, put a piece of wet greaseproof paper on the surface and leave it to cool. Squeeze out
and strain the lemon juice. Put the gelatine in a basin with
the lemon juice and 15 ml (1 tablespoon) cold water and
leave it to dissolve in a pan of gently simmering water. Whisk
the gelatine into the custard and when it is almost setting,
whisk the egg whites until they are stiff but not dry. Fold
the breadcrumbs and cream into the lemon custard, then
gently fold in the egg whites. Turn the mixture into a lightly-
oiled ring mould and leave it to set.

Put the granulated sugar in a pan with 250 ml (½ pint)
cold water and dissolve it gently, then boil it hard for 1
minute. Add the pears to the syrup as soon as they are prepared and poach them gently until they are tender. Split
and stone the plums. Remove the pears from the syrup and

place them on a plate to cool. Poach the plum halves until they are very soft, then drain off the syrup and push them through a sieve to make a thick purée.

To serve, turn the cream out of its mould on to a serving plate and fill the centre with the pears. Coat the cream with the purée and arrange any extra pears, sliced, around the base of the mould. Decorate with cream if you like.

Serves 8

Chinese Toffee Apples

50 g (2 oz) plain flour
2 large cooking apples,
    thickly sliced
oil for deep frying

50 g (2 oz) peanut oil
175 g (6 oz) caster sugar
25 g (1 oz) sesame seeds

Sift the flour into a bowl and pour in, mixing gradually, 60 ml (4 tablespoons) cold water to make a thick batter. Dip the apple pieces in the batter and fry them in the hot oil (199°C (390°F)) for only 2 or 3 minutes, removing them when golden.

Heat the peanut oil with the sugar and 30 ml (2 tablespoons) cold water until the sugar has dissolved. Heat to 163°C(325°F), then immediately drop in some of the apple slices, turn them gently to coat them with toffee and remove with a perforated spoon. Sprinkle with sesame seeds and drop into a bowl of cold water, when the toffee will harden and coat the hot apple in a brilliant, brittle but delicate glaze. Serve at once because the coating softens with waiting.

Serves 4–6

Pear and Chocolate Cream Pie

100 g (4 oz) digestive
  biscuits, crushed
50 g (2 oz) butter, melted
4 large eating pears,
  poached
30 ml (2 level tablespoons)
  cornflour
30 ml (2 level tablespoons)
  cocoa, sifted

250 ml (½ pint) milk
50 g (2 oz) caster sugar
142-g (5-oz) carton double
  cream, whipped
50 g (2 oz) dark chocolate,
  grated

Mix the biscuits with the melted butter and spread this
mixture over the base and sides of a 15-cm (7-in) flan dish,
smoothing the crumbs with the back of a spoon. Leave in
the fridge for 30 minutes to chill and harden.

Cut one or two of the best pear halves into good slices,
lengthwise, for decoration. Blend the cornflour and cocoa
with a little of the milk. Bring the rest to the boil with the
sugar then pour it, stirring, on to the blended mixture.
Return it to the pan and bring it to the boil again, stirring
all the time until the mixture thickens. Cook it gently for
1 minute, then allow it to cool, pressing a piece of wet
greaseproof paper close to the surface to prevent it forming a skin. Don't let it become cold; it only needs to cool
enough so that it won't melt the biscuit crust when it's
poured in.

Chop the remaining pear halves and arrange them in the
flan case. Pour on the chocolate cream and smooth the top
into swirls. Allow to set. Decorate the pie with the pear slices,
arranging them like the spokes of a wheel. Pipe the cream into
rosettes around the dish and in the middle and finish by
sprinkling with the grated chocolate.

Serves 6–8

Teatime

Gathering round the fire for tea after a long Sunday walk or when I've been picking hedgerow fruits is one of my favourite times of the day. That's when the toast should be thick and spread liberally with dripping or honey on the comb, your home-made jam or just plenty of butter. Thick slices of a fruity tea-loaf or fingers of Welsh Rabbit followed by toast and cakes are other alternatives, depending on how strenuous the walk.

You're probably thinking I've made a mistake with my Welsh Rabbit. Not so. Back in the eighteenth century, which is about the earliest reference I can find to this recipe, it was called a rabbit and when you think about it, putting an egg on top of the cheese mixture and then calling it a Buck Rabbit makes sense. During Queen Victoria's reign, somebody decided to tidy up the title for polite society and so it became a rarebit. It's the same dish but I prefer the older name.

Queen Victoria might well have eaten a rarebit, but certainly, later in her life, she became partial to marrow toast and would have it every day for tea – the last thing a fairly

stout lady should include so often in her diet. The recipe
is simple and the results delicious.

Other than occasional family gatherings round the fire,
teatime nowadays is very much a children's meal and so the
majority of recipes in this section will appeal specially to
children – though most of the menfolk I know would prefer
to be included in a meal that consisted of chocolate cup
cakes, waffles or almond cookies.

Fried Cheese Sandwiches

8 thin slices white bread	1 large egg, beaten
50 g (2 oz) butter	30 ml (2 tablespoons) oil
4 slices processed cheese	
30 ml (2 level tablespoons) smooth chutney	

Cut the crusts off the bread and spread each slice with butter. Put a slice of cheese on 4 slices and spread with a quarter
of the chutney. Sandwich with the remaining bread. Mix
30 ml (2 tablespoons) cold water into the egg. Heat the oil
in one frying pan, or divide it between two pans and heat
both. Dip each sandwich quickly in the beaten egg to lightly
coat each side, not to soak them. Fry in the hot oil until one
side is brown, then turn and fry the other side. Cut into
quarters, across the diagonals to make triangles, and pile
them on plates, adding a little cress or a quartered tomato
for garnish.

Serves 4

Fish Paste

225 g (8 oz) poached fish	ground mace
50 g (2 oz) butter, softened	tomato ketchup or
salt and pepper	Worcestershire sauce

Any moist-cooked fish will do such as cod, coley, herring, mackerel or kippers, but you must remove all the skin and bones and flake the fish finely. Then pound it in a bowl using the end of your wooden rolling pin and work it to a paste, adding the butter, a lot of salt and pepper and ground mace and, if you like, some tomato ketchup or Worcestershire sauce, tasting after each addition until the mixture is right. If it's for children, they will probably prefer the tomato ketchup. Either serve with hot toast or spread on bread for sandwiches. If you wish to keep your fish paste, cover it with a layer of melted butter and keep it in the fridge – but only for a few days.

Serves 4

Marrow Toast

2 knuckle-end marrow bones	salt and pepper
4 slices white bread, toasted	15 ml (1 level tablespoon) parsley, chopped
50 g (2 oz) butter	

Cover the open top of each bone with a small piece of foil

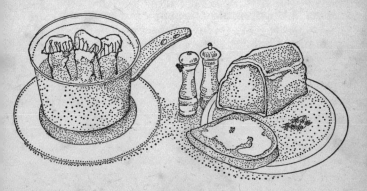

and stand the bones in a saucepan deep enough to pour in water almost up to the foil caps. Bring the water to the boil and simmer the bones for 2 hours. Toast the bread and butter it thickly. Pour the marrow out of the bones on to the toast, sprinkle with salt and pepper and a little parsley and cut into thick fingers.

Serves 4

Hot Dripping Toast

4 slices white bread,   beef dripping
  toasted   salt and pepper

Toast the bread and while it is hot spread it with beef dripping including the jelly from the bottom of the dish. Sprinkle with a little salt and plenty of pepper and serve hot.

Serves 4

Welsh Rabbit

100 g (4 oz) Cheddar   5 ml (1 level teaspoon)
  cheese, grated   mustard powder
30 ml (2 tablespoons)   25 g (1 oz) butter
  brown ale   2 slices white bread,
salt and pepper   toasted

Put the cheese and ale in a pan and heat gently to melt the cheese. Season the mixture well with salt and pepper and the mustard and beat in the butter. When it is thoroughly hot, spread the mixture on the toast and return the toast to the grill until the topping is bubbling and golden brown in places.

Serves 2

Marshmallow Shortcake

100 g (4 oz) butter
100 g (4 oz) caster sugar
3 ml (½ teaspoon) vanilla
   essence
1 large egg, beaten
225 g (8 oz) plain flour
5 ml (1 level teaspoon)
   baking powder

Marshmallow:
20 ml (2 level dessertspoons)
   powdered gelatine
175 g (6 oz) caster sugar
1 large egg white
175 g (6 oz) icing sugar,
   sifted

50 g (2 oz) chopped mixed
   nuts, toasted

Cream the butter and sugar until they are light and fluffy, then beat in the vanilla essence. Beat in the egg, then sift in the flour and baking powder and mix gently. Turn the dough on to greaseproof paper and roll it to a 1.25-cm (½-in) thick round. Transfer, still on the paper, to a baking tray and bake it at 180°C(350°F)/Gas 4 for about 30 minutes or until golden. Leave to cool.

Put the gelatine in a saucepan with 180 ml (12 tablespoons) cold water and heat it very gently until it has dissolved. Then add the caster sugar, stir until it dissolves, bring it to the boil and boil for 8 minutes. Allow to cool. Whisk the egg white until it is stiff, then fold in the icing sugar. Slowly pour on the cooled gelatine mixture, beating all the time, and continue beating for about 3 minutes until the icing is white and thick. Spread over the cold shortbread and sprinkle with the nuts.

Serves 6

Chocolate Cup Cakes

100 g (4 oz) butter
75 g (3 oz) caster sugar
2 large eggs, beaten
100 g (4 oz) plain
 chocolate, melted
75 g (3 oz) self-raising flour
25 g (1 oz) rice flour

Chocolate frosting:
150 g (5 oz) icing sugar,
 sifted
1 standard egg, beaten
25 g (1 oz) plain chocolate,
 melted
25 g (1 oz) butter

Cream the butter and caster sugar until they are light and fluffy. Alternately beat in the eggs and melted but cooled chocolate, then fold in the flour and rice flour, sifted together. Divide the mixture between paper cake cases standing in deep patty tins. Bake at 180°C(350°F)/Gas 4 for 15–20 minutes until well risen and springy to touch. Turn out of the patty tins on to a rack to cool.

Put all the ingredients for the frosting into a bowl and stand the bowl over a pan of gently simmering water. Make sure the base of the bowl isn't touching the water and whisk the mixture until it is very light and fluffy. Spoon a good layer of icing over each cup cake, allow it to settle on its own, then leave to set.

Makes 16

Cinnamon Toast

4 slices white bread, toasted
25 g (1 oz) butter

50 g (2 oz) granulated
 sugar
ground cinnamon

Spread the toasted bread with butter and coat each slice with a little of the sugar. Sprinkle well with ground cinnamon and put the toast back under the grill for a few minutes until the sugar topping is crunchy. Eat hot.

Serves 4

Chocolate Crackle Flan

50 g (2 oz) plain chocolate,
  melted
knob of butter
100 g (4 oz) rice cereal
250 ml (½ pint) milk

30 marshmallows
250 ml (½ pint) double
  cream
peppermint essence

Mix the chocolate, butter and rice cereal together until the rice is well coated with chocolate. Turn it into a deep 20-cm (8-in) dish and smooth it along the top with the back of a spoon. Put it in the fridge to chill and set. Pour the milk into a double saucepan or put it in a basin standing in a pan of gently-simmering water. Add the marshmallows and stir gently while heating until they have melted. Half-whip the cream and fold it gently into the cooled marshmallow mixture with enough peppermint essence to flavour the mixture well. If liked, add a few drops of green colouring at the same time. Pour this mixture into the case, swirl the top and leave it to set.

Serves 6–8

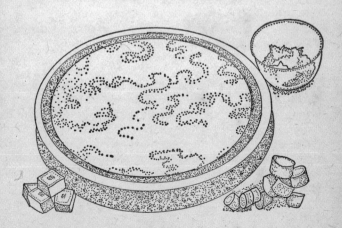

Butterscotch Pear Trifle

4 trifle sponge cakes
4 large pears, poached
1 large lemon

500-ml (1-pint) packet
butterscotch instant
dessert
500 ml (1 pint) milk

Cut the sponge cakes into small pieces and soak them with the syrup in which the pears were poached. (For an even quicker pudding for tea, use canned pears.) Finely grate the rind from the lemon and squeeze out and strain the juice. Pour the juice over the sponges and sprinkle on the lemon rind. Top with the pear halves. Whisk the butterscotch instant dessert with the milk and when it is on the point of setting, swirl it over the pears with a knife to make an attractive finish. Chill for 10–30 minutes before serving.

Serves 6–8

Blackberry and Apple Dumplings

0.5 kg (1 lb) cooking apples,
thickly sliced
225 g (8 oz) blackberries
100 g (4 oz) granulated
sugar

100 g (4 oz) self-raising
flour
50 g (2 oz) shredded suet

Put the apples with the blackberries and granulated sugar in a pan. Add 125 ml ($\frac{1}{4}$ pint) cold water. Sift the flour, stir in the suet and mix to a soft dough with cold water. Form the dough into small dumplings. Heat the fruit to simmering point and lower in the dumplings. Cover the pan with a tight-fitting lid and simmer the dumplings for 10–15 minutes. Remove them on to hot serving dishes, stir the fruit and spoon it over.

Serves 6

Anytime Chocolate Biscuits

75 g (3 oz) butter
75 g (3 oz) caster sugar
1 large egg, beaten

165 g (6½ oz) self-raising
flour
15 g (½ oz) cocoa powder

Cream the butter and sugar until they are light and fluffy,
then beat in the egg. Sift the flour with the cocoa powder
and stir it into the mixture. Chill. Form the dough into a roll
without adding any extra flour. The easiest way is to put it
in a sheet of greaseproof paper and roll it under the palms
of your hands on a wooden board. Over-wrap in foil and
leave the mixture in the fridge until you need it. If you want
to keep the dough for longer than a couple of days, put it
in the freezer, but allow it to thaw just sufficiently to cut it
into thin slices. When ready to eat the biscuits, slice the roll
thinly, arrange the biscuits on greased baking trays and bake
them at 200°C(400°F)/Gas 6 for 8–10 minutes. Allow to cool.

Makes 30

Flaky Pinwheels

213-g (7½-oz) packet frozen
puff pastry, thawed
30 ml (2 level tablespoons)
apricot jam
50 g (2 oz) chopped mixed
nuts

1 small egg white, lightly
whisked
caster sugar

Roll the pastry on a lightly-floured board until it is very
thin, trying to keep it a good oblong shape. Trim the edges.
Brush the pastry with the apricot jam, leaving a narrow strip
of pastry around two short edges and one long one. Sprinkle
with the nuts and brush the pastry edges with water. Roll
the pastry like a Swiss roll from the long jam-covered edge,
pressing the moistened edges to seal them. Using a very
sharp knife, cut the roll into 24 biscuits and arrange them on

greased baking trays, reshaping them if necessary into a round again. Brush them with some of the egg white and sprinkle them with some caster sugar. Bake them at 200°C(400°F)/Gas 6 for 15–20 minutes or until they are golden and crisp, brushing them half-way through the cooking with the rest of the egg and sprinkling them again with sugar.

Makes 24

Honey Crisps

75 g (3 oz) butter
45 ml (3 level tablespoons) honey

40 g (1½ oz) Demerara sugar
100 g (4 oz) rice cereal

Heat the butter, honey and sugar gently until the sugar has melted, then stir in the rice cereal thoroughly to coat it well. Press this into a large buttered Swiss roll tin and smooth the top. Bake at 160°C(325°F)/Gas 3 for about 20 minutes. Remove from the oven, allow to cool slightly, then cut the crisps into squares and loosen them from the edges of the tin. Remove from the tin when they have cooled enough to handle easily.

Makes 24

Quick Chocolate Fingers

100 g (4 oz) butter
25 g (1 oz) caster sugar
50 g (2 oz) drinking chocolate
15 ml (1 level tablespoon) golden syrup

225 g (8 oz) digestive biscuits, crushed
50 g (2 oz) sultanas

Melt the butter and stir in the sugar with the drinking chocolate, sifted if lumpy, and the golden syrup and beat well. Stir in the crushed biscuits and sultanas and press the mixture into a greased, small Swiss roll tin. Allow to set, then cut into fingers.

Makes 16

Plum Delicious

4 thin slices white bread   8 large plums
50 g (2 oz) butter   50 g (2 oz) Demerara sugar

Cut the crusts off the bread and arrange the slices on a greased baking tray. Butter thickly. Cut the plums in half and remove the stones. Arrange 4 halves on each bread slice, cut side up, and sprinkle thickly with the sugar. Bake them at 180°C(350°F)/Gas 4 for 10–15 minutes or until the sugar has turned to a rich caramel and the bread is crisp and golden.

Serves 4

Poor Knights of Windsor

8 1.25-cm (½-in) thick   1 large egg, beaten
   slices of white bread   50 g (2 oz) butter
250 ml (½ pint) milk   60 ml (4 level tablespoons)
50 g (2 oz) caster sugar   strawberry jam

Cut the crusts off the bread. Beat the milk, sugar and egg together and pour it into a flat dish or plate. Dip the bread slices quickly in this mixture, just to coat them not to soak them, and put them immediately into the hot butter in a frying pan and fry until the bread is golden on both sides. Spread quickly with the jam, cut into fingers and serve at once.

Serves 4

Feather-light Scones

225 g (8 oz) self-raising
  flour
5 ml (1 level teaspoon)
  baking powder

3 ml ($\frac{1}{2}$ level teaspoon) salt
50 g (2 oz) butter
125 ml ($\frac{1}{4}$ pint) milk

Sift the flour, baking powder and salt into a bowl. Rub in the butter and, using a knife, mix with the milk to make a soft but not sticky dough. Turn the mixture on to a lightly-floured board and knead it lightly until smooth. Roll out to a 1.75-cm ($\frac{3}{4}$-in) thickness and cut out 10 scones using a 6-cm ($2\frac{1}{2}$-in) fluted cutter. Arrange them on a greased baking tray and bake them at 230°C(450°F)/Gas 8 for 8–10 minutes or until golden. Cool on a wire rack and serve with butter or jam and cream.

Makes 10

Almond Cookies

200 g (8 oz) butter
200 g (8 oz) caster sugar
125 g (5 oz) plain flour

100 g (4 oz) almonds,
  finely chopped

Cream the butter and sugar until they are light and fluffy, then sift in the flour and, using your hands, work it into the mixture with the almonds, until it is smooth. Form the mixture into a roll about 5 cm (2 in) in diameter and wrap it in greaseproof paper. Leave it in the fridge for 2 hours to chill and become firm, then cut the roll into about 30 biscuits. Arrange them on lightly-greased baking trays and bake them at 180°C(350°F)/Gas 4 for about 10 minutes. Cool on wire racks. These have a funny shape but a wonderful flavour.

Makes 30

Spicy Refrigerator Biscuits

100 g (4 oz) butter
150 g (6 oz) caster sugar
1 large egg, beaten
250 g (10 oz) plain flour
3 ml (½ level teaspoon)
 bicarbonate of soda
3 ml (½ level teaspoon)
 baking powder

pinch of salt
10 ml (2 level teaspoons)
 ground cinnamon
142-g (5-oz) carton soured
 cream
icing sugar, sifted

Cream the butter and sugar until they are light and fluffy.
Beat in the egg. Sift the flour with the bicarbonate of soda,
baking powder, salt and cinnamon and stir it alternately
into the creamed mixture with the soured cream. Leave the
dough overnight in the fridge, covering the bowl with a
cloth.

Next day, roll the dough on a lightly-floured board and
cut it into rounds using a 6-cm (2½-in) fluted cutter. Place on
ungreased baking trays and bake them at 190°C(375°F)/
Gas 5 for about 15–20 minutes or until lightly browned.
Turn on to a wire rack to cool, then sprinkle with icing sugar.

Makes 30

Drop Scones

3 ml (½ level teaspoon)
 bicarbonate of soda
250 ml (½ pint) buttermilk
225 g (8 oz) plain flour

pinch of salt
1 large egg, beaten
25 g (1 oz) lard

Stir the bicarbonate of soda into the buttermilk. Sift the
flour and salt into a bowl and make a well in the centre. Add
the egg and buttermilk and beat well for about 5 minutes.
Grease a heavy frying pan with a little of the lard and drop
15 ml (1 tablespoon) of the mixture for each scone into the

pan. Cook for 2 minutes or until golden, then turn each one
and cook again for about 1 minute. Keep them hot while
you cook the rest of the mixture. Serve hot with butter and
sugar or golden syrup.

Makes 30

Waffles with Maple Syrup

175 g (6 oz) plain flour
pinch of salt
15 ml (1 level tablespoon)
   baking powder
25 g (1 oz) caster sugar

2 large eggs, separated
250 ml (½ pint) milk
50 g (2 oz) butter, melted
maple syrup

Sift the flour, salt and baking powder into a bowl, stir in the
sugar and make a well in the centre. Add the egg yolks and
mix in with the milk and melted butter, added alternately.
Whisk the egg whites until they are stiff but not dry and fold
them in lightly. Pour a little of the batter into a heated
waffle iron, close the iron and cook the waffle for 2–3
minutes, turning it once. The waffles should be golden
brown and crisp; if any stick, cook them for a little longer.
If you need to keep them hot while you finish the rest of the
batter, stand them on a wire rack. Stacking them only
makes them soggy. Serve hot with maple syrup poured over.
They are also good with melted butter or golden syrup.

Makes 16

Parties

We may not be into the real swing of the party season yet, but there are two occasions in autumn which are very important. Of course, I'm referring to Guy Fawkes, which is celebrated by most families, and Hallowe'en, which gives a marvellous excuse for all things spooky.

Both kinds of party require chunky foods which can be eaten with the fingers, hot and hearty for those who have been standing around getting cold watching rockets soar over next door's garden. And food should be the simplest kind but made in large quantities. For this reason there are few of the handing-round kind of titbits included here, but more of the dishes like Lasagne, Chilli con Carne and Curry to give an inner glow to toes and fingers. Bangers and mash, simple but good, is the perfect fare for this kind of party, and I've given another couple of ways with sausages – served in blankets and as a plait. Fried chicken drumsticks, crisply-coated and spiced with mustard, can be eaten indoors or out or a mixture of both depending on the weather. And don't forget the versatility of jacket potatoes (page 14), just right for a cold autumn night. Cakes can certainly be included in the menu and gingerbread, and devil's food mixtures are appropriate, though not to be thought of as once-a-year treats. Once you've tried these recipes, you'll need no excuse to serve them again.

Sausage Plait

369-g (13-oz) packet frozen puff pastry, thawed
225 g (½ lb) pork sausagemeat
1 large egg, beaten
1 large onion, grated
5 ml (1 level teaspoon) mixed dried herbs
15 ml (1 level tablespoon) tomato ketchup
salt and pepper

Roll the pastry on a lightly-floured board until it is very thin and a good oblong shape. Trim the edges to make a perfect oblong. Mix the sausagemeat with the egg (keeping a little in reserve for brushing the pastry), grated onion, herbs, ketchup and seasoning. Form into a roll almost as long as the pastry, flouring your hands if necessary. Place the sausagemeat down the centre of the pastry. Using a sharp knife, make diagonal cuts down each side of the pastry cutting it into 1.25-cm (½-in) strips. Moisten the ends of the pastry on both sides and fold the strips alternately across the sausagemeat to make a plait. Transfer it to a wet baking tray and brush the pastry with the reserved egg. Bake it at 220°C(425°F)/Gas 7 for 25–30 minutes or until the pastry is well puffed and golden brown. Cut into slices to serve.

Serves 4–8

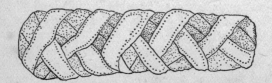

Sausages in Blankets

200 g (8 oz) shortcrust
  pastry (see page 54)
10 ml (1 level dessertspoon)
  made mustard

0.5 kg (1 lb) thick pork or
  beef sausages
1 small egg, beaten

Roll the shortcrust pastry on a lightly-floured board and cut
into 8 squares, each one large enough to almost enclose a
sausage. Spread the middle of each square with a little of
the mustard. Separate the sausages and lay one on each
piece of pastry across the diagonal. Wrap 2 points around
each sausage, securing them by moistening one with a little
water and pressing it to the other. Arrange the sausages on
a greased baking tray and brush each with a little of the egg.
Bake at 200°C(400°F)/Gas 6 for 25–30 minutes or until the
pastry is golden brown.

Serves 4–8

Chilli con Carne

675 g (1½ lb) red kidney
  beans
pinch of bicarbonate of
  soda
30 ml (2 tablespoons) oil
1.5 kg (3 lb) minced beef
2 large onions, roughly
  chopped
2 large green peppers,
  roughly chopped

1 kg (2 lb) ripe tomatoes,
  skinned
salt and pepper
20 ml (2 level dessertspoons)
  chilli powder
30 ml (2 tablespoons)
  vinegar

Put the kidney beans in a bowl which will hold twice their
volume, because they swell during soaking. Cover them with
plenty of cold water and add the pinch of bicarbonate of
soda. Leave to soak overnight.

Next day, heat the oil in a large pan and fry the beef gently until it has browned all over. Add the onion and pepper and fry for a further 5–10 minutes. Drain the beans well and stir them into the meat. Chop the tomatoes and add to the mixture and season it very well with salt and pepper and the chilli powder. Stir in the vinegar. Transfer the mixture to 1 or 2 large casserole dishes, cover them with lids and cook them slowly at 160°C(325°F)/Gas 3 for 2½–3 hours or until the beans are tender.

Serves 12

Lamb Curry

1.5 kg (3 lb) shoulder of lamb
50 g (2 oz) butter
2 large onions, roughly chopped
2 cloves garlic, roughly chopped
1 large cooking apple, chopped
5 ml (1 level teaspoon) chilli powder
30 ml (2 level tablespoons) curry paste
20 ml (2 level dessertspoons) tomato paste
salt and pepper

Remove any excess fat from the lamb and cut the meat into bite-sized chunks. Heat the butter in a pan and fry the onion and garlic for 5 minutes, then add the apple and continue to fry for another 3 minutes. Stir in the chilli and curry paste for 2 minutes more, then add the meat and stir until the meat is brown on all sides. Stir in the tomato paste and 500 ml (1 pint) cold water, or stock if you have it, and bring to the boil. Lower the heat, cover the pan and simmer for 2 hours or until the meat is tender. Check the seasoning, adding a little salt and pepper if necessary. Serve with accompaniments such as those listed below.

Serves 8–12

Curry Accompaniments

Poppadums
You can buy these in flat cardboard boxes from good grocers. Heat about 1.25 cm ($\frac{1}{2}$ in) oil in a frying pan until it is very hot. Put in one poppadum, hold it down with a fish slice to keep it flat and watch it enlarge immediately and darken slightly. Remove at once and stand it on its edge on plenty of crumpled kitchen paper so that the excess oil can drip off. This is easier when you have a few made and they support each other. Don't overcook them, 4–5 seconds is ample. Allow 1 or 2 per person.

Banana and Raisins
Peel 4 large bananas and cut them into thinnish slices, slightly on the diagonal instead of straight across. Toss them immediately in the strained juice of 1 lemon then mix with 100 g (4 oz) seedless or stoned raisins.

Cucumber Raita
Peel and cut 1 cucumber into small dice. Lightly beat two 142-g (5-oz) cartons plain yoghurt with a little cold water, if necessary, to make a thin pouring consistency. Finely chop 10 ml (2 level teaspoons) mint and mix into the yoghurt with the cucumber dice. Season with salt and pepper and chill.

Tomato Soup with Herb Dumplings

1 kg (2 lb) very ripe
  tomatoes, quartered
salt and pepper
250 ml ($\frac{1}{2}$ pint) chicken
  stock
5 ml (1 level teaspoon)
  caster sugar

Herb dumplings:
100 g (4 oz) self-raising
  flour, sifted
50 g (2 oz) shredded suet
$\frac{1}{2}$ small onion, finely grated
5 ml (1 level teaspoon)
  mixed dried herbs
salt and pepper

Put the tomatoes in a large pan and season them with salt

and pepper. Cover with a tightly-fitting lid and simmer them very slowly for 20 minutes or until they are very soft. Push them through a sieve to make a purée and return the purée to the rinsed pan. Pour in the stock and add the sugar.

Meanwhile, mix the flour for the dumplings with the shredded suet, onion, herbs and a good pinch each of salt and pepper. Mix to a soft dough with cold water. Flour your hands and form the mixture into lots of little dumplings, each about the size of a walnut.

Bring the soup to the boil, drop the dumplings into it, cover the pan with the lid, lower the heat and simmer the dumplings for 20 minutes or until well risen and fluffy. Check the seasoning in the soup and serve piping hot.

Serves 6

Cheese Straws

100 g (4 oz) plain flour, sifted	50 g (2 oz) butter
pinch of salt	50 g (2 oz) Cheddar cheese, grated
good pinch of cayenne pepper	1 egg yolk

Mix the flour with the salt and cayenne pepper and rub in the butter. Stir in the cheese and mix to a stiff dough with the egg yolk and a little cold water. Roll the pastry on a lightly-floured board until it is fairly thin, though thicker than you would like for a pastry crust, trying to keep it to a good oblong shape. Cut it into oblongs 7.5 cm (3 in) wide and cut each oblong into straws about 0.5 cm ($\frac{1}{4}$ in) wide. Arrange the straws on greased baking trays and bake them at 200°C(400°F)/Gas 6 for 10–15 minutes or until pale golden brown. Transfer to a wire rack to cool.

Another version uses scraps of puff pastry. Stack the trimmings on top of each other, rather than gathering them into a ball, and roll the pastry thinly. Sprinkle it with cayenne pepper and grated Parmesan cheese and cut into strips as above. Twist each strip and arrange on a baking tray. Bake at 230°C(450°F)/Gas 8 for about 10 minutes or until puffed and golden. Serve hot or allow to cool on a wire rack.

Makes 40

Bangers and Mash

454-g (1-lb) packet thick pork sausages
450 g (1 lb) potatoes, prepared
salt

1 large onion, roughly chopped
pepper
25 g (1 oz) butter

Separate the sausages and put them in a frying pan and fry them very gently at first until the fat begins to run, then increase the heat slightly and continue to cook them, turning them frequently, until they are cooked through and brown on all sides.

Meanwhile, cut the potatoes into small chunks and put them in a pan of salted water. Bring to the boil and cook them for 15 minutes or until they are soft enough to mash. Put the onion in a small pan, just cover it with cold water and bring it to the boil. Lower the heat and cook the onion for 15–20 minutes or until it is soft and tender. Drain the potatoes and the onion. Mash the potatoes well, beating in salt and pepper, the butter and the onion pieces. Pile it on a serving plate.

Drain the sausages and arrange them round the potato. Serve hot with plenty of accompaniments such as home-made chutney, mustard, pickle or horseradish sauce.

Serves 4–6

Lasagne

1 large onion, finely
   chopped
15 ml (1 tablespoon) oil
675 g (1½ lb) raw mince
2 425-g (15-oz) cans
   tomatoes
pinch of dried basil
salt and pepper
375 g (12 oz) green lasagne

50 g (2 oz) butter
50 g (2 oz) plain flour
500 ml (1 pint) milk
ground nutmeg
100 g (4 oz) Cheddar
   cheese, grated
50 g (2 oz) Parmesan
   cheese, grated

Fry the onion in the oil for 5 minutes, then add the mince and fry it, stirring often, until it is brown on all sides. Put the tomatoes and their juice in a saucepan and break them down with a wooden spoon. Bring to the boil and simmer them for 30 minutes with the basil and plenty of salt and pepper. Season the mince with salt and pepper and continue to cook it slowly for a further 30 minutes, adding 250 ml (½ pint) cold water. Cook the lasagne according to the packet instructions and drain it well.

Melt the butter in a pan, stir in the flour and cook the mixture for 1 minute. Remove from the heat and gradually stir in the milk. Return the pan to the heat and bring to the boil, stirring all the time, then simmer for 2 minutes, stirring frequently. Season the sauce with salt and pepper and some ground nutmeg.

Arrange the pasta, tomato sauce, meat and white sauce in layers, in this order, in a deep ovenproof dish, ending with a thick layer of white sauce. Mix the cheeses together and sprinkle them all over the top and cook the lasagne in the oven at 190°C(375°F)/Gas 5 for 30 minutes or until the top is golden brown and bubbling. If you have to keep lasagne waiting, turn down the oven to its very lowest setting and cover the dish with a piece of foil.

Serves 8–12

Fried Chicken Drumsticks

8 chicken drumsticks	2 cloves garlic, finely
salt and pepper	chopped
50 g (2 oz) fresh white	1 large egg, beaten
breadcrumbs	oil for deep frying

Wipe the chicken drumsticks and season them with salt and pepper. Season the breadcrumbs with salt and pepper and mix with the garlic. Coat each drumstick first in beaten egg, then in the breadcrumbs, patting them on well. Put the chicken pieces on a plate and leave them in the fridge until you are ready to fry them. Heat the oil to 182°C(360°F) and fry the drumsticks, a few at a time, until they are golden brown and cooked through. Serve hot with the bones wrapped in paper napkins.

Serves 8

Walnut Cream Roll

4 large eggs	25 g (1 oz) butter, melted
75 g (3 oz) caster sugar	1 large eating apple,
40 g (1½ oz) plain flour,	chopped
sifted	225 g (8 oz) blackberries
40 g (1½ oz) walnut halves,	100 g (4 oz) granulated sugar
ground	250 ml (½ pint) double
pinch of ground nutmeg	cream, whipped

Whisk the eggs with the caster sugar in a bowl standing over a pan of hot water. When they are thick and fluffy, fold in the flour, walnuts, and melted butter. Spread the mixture lightly in a 25×38-cm (10×15-in) Swiss roll tin, lined with greased greaseproof paper. Bake it at 190°C(375°F)/Gas 5 for 10 minutes or until it has shrunk slightly from the edges of the tin and is springy when touched lightly. Lay a sheet of greaseproof paper on a work surface and sprinkle it with caster sugar. Turn out the sponge on to this.

Meanwhile, simmer the apple pieces with the blackberries and granulated sugar until they are soft. Chill this mixture in the fridge. Trim the edges off the cake and spread it with half of the whipped cream. Spread with the fruit mixture and roll the sponge carefully from the long sides. If you find this difficult, simply fold it in three like an omelette. Cover the top with a coating of the cream and put the remainder in a piping bag fitted with a large star pipe. Decorate with cream stars and if you have some good blackberries, add a few to the top.

Serves 6–8

Devil's Food Cake

175 g (6 oz) soft, whipped margarine

175 g (6 oz) caster sugar

175 g (6 oz) plain flour, sifted

175 g (6 oz) golden syrup

2 large eggs, beaten

50 g (2 oz) ground almonds

25 g (1 oz) cocoa powder, sifted

3 ml (½ level teaspoon) bicarbonate of soda

125 ml (¼ pint) milk

Chocolate fudge icing:

75 g (3 oz) butter

50 g (2 oz) cocoa powder, sifted

90 ml (6 tablespoons) evaporated milk

225 g (8 oz) icing sugar, sifted

Put all the ingredients for the cake, except the bicarbonate of soda and milk, in a bowl. Dissolve the bicarbonate of soda in the milk, then add it to the bowl and beat with a wooden spoon until smooth, adding a little more milk if necessary to make a soft dropping consistency. Turn the mixture into a well-greased and lined 20-cm (8-in) square cake tin with a fixed base and bake it at 150°C(300°F)/Gas 2 for about 1¾ hours until a skewer comes out clean and the cake has slightly shrunk from the edges of the tin. Allow to cool for 5 minutes in the tin, then turn the cake on to a wire rack and peel off the lining paper.

Melt the butter for the icing in a pan and stir in the cocoa, then cook the mixture for 1 minute over a gentle heat. Remove from the heat and stir in the evaporated milk and icing sugar and beat well until the icing is smooth and shiny. Allow to cool.

Wrap a collar of greaseproof paper tightly around the cake. Lightly oil a 2.5-cm (1-in) band around the top edge of the collar. Pour the cooled icing over the cake and allow it to set. Peel off the paper collar very carefully so the icing is not disturbed. Cut the cake into squares to serve.

Makes 16

Banana Rum Ring

100 g (4 oz) plain flour
5 ml (1 level teaspoon)
  baking powder
100 g (4 oz) butter
100 g (4 oz) caster sugar
2 large eggs, beaten

60 ml (4 level tablespoons)
  golden syrup
15 ml (1 tablespoon)
  rum
3 large bananas, sliced
juice of 1 lemon, strained

Sift the flour and baking powder. Cream the butter and sugar until the mixture is light and fluffy. Then beat in the eggs, a little at a time. Fold in the flour, using a large tablespoon. Turn the mixture into a greased and floured 18-cm (7-in) ring tin and bake it at 190°C(375°F)/Gas 5 for 20–25 minutes or until the cake is springy to touch and has shrunk slightly from the edges of the tin. Invert the tin on to a wire rack and leave it to cool. The cake will drop out of the tin as it cools.

Heat the golden syrup with 30 ml (2 tablespoons) cold

water in a saucepan and when hot add the rum. Prick the sponge all over with a darning needle and spoon over the rum syrup, collecting any that doesn't soak straight in on a plate underneath. Keep pouring the syrup over until the sponge has absorbed it all.

Toss the bananas in the lemon juice to prevent them discolouring and pile them into the centre to serve. Add whipped cream, if liked.

Serves 6–8

Ovaltine Fruit Loaf

200 g (7 oz) self-raising
    flour
25 g (1 oz) Ovaltine
50 g (2 oz) brown sugar

100 g (4 oz) chopped dates
75 g (3 oz) golden syrup
125 ml ($\frac{1}{4}$ pint) milk

Sift the flour and Ovaltine into a mixing bowl, then add the rest of the ingredients and beat well. Turn the mixture into a well greased 0.5-kg (1-lb) loaf tin and bake at 180°C(350°F)/ Gas 4 for 50 minutes or until the loaf is golden brown and has shrunk slightly from the edges of the tin. Allow to cool for 5 minutes in the tin, then turn on to a wire rack to cool. Cut into thick slices and serve well buttered.

Serves 8–12

Greengage Lattice

150 g (6 oz) shortcrust
    pastry (see page 54)
675 g (1$\frac{1}{2}$ lb) greengages

75 g (3 oz) granulated sugar
10 ml (2 level teaspoons)
    arrowroot

Roll the pastry on a lightly-floured board and use it to line a 20-cm (8-in) flan dish. Trim the edge and leave it in the fridge to rest.

Halve the greengages and remove the stones. Put them in a pan with 125 ml (¼ pint) cold water and the sugar. Simmer until the sugar has dissolved, then poach the greengages until they are soft but not breaking up. Remove from the syrup and drain them well. Allow to cool before filling the flan with them. Roll the remaining pieces of pastry, cut them into strips and use them to make a lattice across the greengages, sticking the ends to the flan with a little water. Bake the flan at 200°C(400°F)/Gas 6 for 25–30 minutes or until the pastry is golden brown.

Meanwhile, blend the arrowroot with a little of the syrup and pour it into the pan. Bring the syrup to the boil, stirring all the time, and cook for 1 minute until it is thick and clear. Spoon the syrup over the greengages when the flan comes out of the oven and serve hot or cold.

Serves 6–8

Anzacs

50 g (2 oz) plain flour, sifted
75 g (3 oz) caster sugar
50 g (2 oz) desiccated coconut
50 g (2 oz) porridge oats
50 g (2 oz) butter

15 ml (1 level tablespoon) golden syrup
3 ml (½ level teaspoon) bicarbonate of soda
30 ml (2 tablespoons) boiling water

Mix together the flour, sugar, coconut and oats. Melt the butter and golden syrup in a saucepan, then dissolve the bicarbonate of soda in the boiling water and add to the butter mixture. Make a well in the centre of the dry ingredients, pour in the butter mixture and stir well to mix. Place spoonfuls of the mixture on greased baking trays, allowing room for spreading, and bake at 180°C(350°F)/Gas 4 for 10–15 minutes.

Makes 20

Gingerbread

350 g (12 oz) plain flour
5 ml (1 level teaspoon)
  bicarbonate of soda
100 g (4 oz) fine oatmeal
225 g (8 oz) butter
60 ml (4 tablespoons)
  single cream

350 g (12 oz) black treacle
25 g (1 oz) fresh root
  ginger
100 g (4 oz) candied lemon
  peel

Sift the flour and bicarbonate of soda into a bowl and stir in
the oatmeal. Cream the butter until it is very light and fluffy,
then beat in the flour mixture alternately with the cream.
Heat the treacle until it is just runny but not too hot. Peel
the fresh ginger and cut it and the lemon peel into fine
shreds. Add the treacle, ginger and lemon peel to the bowl
and mix well. Turn the mixture into a greased 25×30-cm
(10×12-in) tin and bake it at 160°C(325°F)/Gas 3 for 45–50
minutes. Allow to cool, then cut into squares.

Makes 16

Doughnuts

225 g (8 oz) plain flour
3 ml (½ level teaspoon)
  bicarbonate of soda
5 ml (1 level teaspoon)
  cream of tartar
pinch of ground nutmeg
pinch of salt

25 g (1 oz) butter, softened
50 g (2 oz) caster sugar
1 large egg, beaten
milk to mix
oil for deep frying
25 g (1 oz) granulated sugar

Sift the flour, bicarbonate of soda, cream of tartar, salt and
nutmeg into a bowl. Rub in the butter and stir in the sugar and
mix with the egg and a little milk to give a fairly stiff dough,
one you can roll out. Turn the dough on to a lightly-
floured board and roll it to a 1.25-cm (½-in) thickness. Heat

the oil to 188°C(370°F) or until a 2.5-cm (1-in) cube of bread will brown in 1 minute. Cut the dough into rounds using a 7.5-cm (3-in) plain cutter, then cut out the middles using a 2.5-cm (1-in) plain cutter. Reroll the middles and cut more rounds or fry them as little doughnuts. Deep fry a few of the doughnuts at a time until they are golden brown, turning them frequently. Drain on crumpled kitchen paper, sprinkle with granulated sugar and serve at once.

Makes 6–7

Pastries

Look in any baker's shop window and you'll find the kind of cakes for which I've given recipes in this chapter. Not all of them are made with pastry, but I've used the title Pastries rather than Baking to indicate the smaller, fancier and daintier type of cakes. A special occasion to most of us means a box of cream cakes, Dad's favourite, one each for the children (all the same to try and prevent squabbles) and one for us. And although it's certainly far quicker to nip down to the baker's for your selection, you can make the very same kind of thing at home. When you hold a bought cake in your hand and it's covered with icing, filled with cream and possibly decorated as well, you might imagine that it took a very complicated process and required skills which only the best pastry cooks possess. I don't think this is so and all the methods given here are simple. Many of these pastries will store well in air-tight tins. Others can be frozen to be filled and finished later, so you can divide your labours and your costs.

Russian Cigarettes

115 g (4½ oz) butter,
  softened

200 g (7 oz) icing sugar,
  sifted

140 g (5½ oz) plain flour,
  sifted

4 large egg whites

Make sure the butter is really soft and creamy, then work in
the sugar. Mix in the flour and when it's well blended, beat
in the egg whites and continue to beat until the mixture is very
smooth. Drop a little of the mixture from the end of a 5-ml
spoon (1 teaspoon) on to a well buttered baking tray,
leaving plenty of space between each mound to allow for
spreading. Bake them at 180°C(350°F)/Gas 4 for 8–10
minutes or until the edges are just beginning to colour.
Remove them from the oven and while they are still hot,
take them off the tray with a palette knife, roll each one
quickly round a pencil and put them on a wire rack to cool.
When cold they are very fragile and crisp.

Makes 50

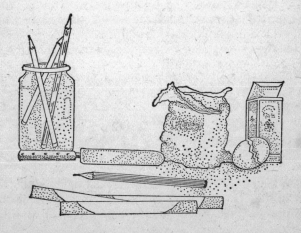

Almond Crescents

125 g (5 oz) ground
    almonds
125 g (5 oz) icing sugar,
    sifted
15 ml (1 level tablespoon)
    apricot jam

2 large egg whites, lightly
    whisked
plain flour
50 g (2 oz) fine flaked
    almonds

Mix the ground almonds with the icing sugar, then work in
the apricot jam. Bit by bit, work in the egg whites until you
have a paste which you can roll with your fingers on the
work surface. If you have some egg white left over, you will
use this later. Divide the paste into pieces the size of walnut
shells and roll them into a sausage shape. You may need a
little plain flour to help you but use the barest minimum.
Moisten each one with a little left-over egg white (or use a
little beaten whole egg) and roll it in the flaked almonds.
If the almond flakes are very large, you may have to chop
them a little, but don't make them too fine. Shape each
finger into a crescent and arrange it on non-stick paper on a
baking tray. Brush the tops lightly with a little egg and bake
them at 180°C(350°F)/Gas 4 for about 15 minutes or until
they are golden brown. Remove from the oven, loosen each
one from the paper and transfer them to a wire rack to cool.

Makes 18

Langues de Chat

50 g (2 oz) butter
50 g (2 oz) caster sugar
1 standard egg, beaten

50 g (2 oz) self-raising
    flour, sifted

Cream the butter and sugar until they are light and fluffy.
Beat in the egg, then work in the flour to make a piping
consistency. Chill. Spoon into a piping bag fitted with

a 1.25-cm ($\frac{1}{2}$-in) plain pipe and pipe fingers, 6–8 cm ($2\frac{1}{2}$–3-in) long, on to greased baking trays. Space them well to allow for a little spreading. Bake at 220°C(425°F)/Gas 7 for about 5 minutes or until the edges of the biscuits are beginning to colour. Cool on a wire rack. These biscuits are often served with rich sweets such as syllabub or zabaglione.

Makes 24

Jam Tarts

150 g (6 oz) shortcrust
  pastry (see page 54)

120 ml (8 level tablespoons)
  jam

Roll the pastry on a lightly-floured board and using a 7.5-cm (3-in) fluted cutter, cut out 12 rounds and press the rounds into 12 greased tartlet tins. Add 10 ml (1 heaped teaspoon) of jam to each tart and bake them at 200°C 400°F)/Gas 6 for 15–20 minutes or until the pastry is golden. Cool on a wire rack.

Makes 12

Oat Thins

25 g (1 oz) butter
100 g (4 oz) caster sugar
1 large egg, beaten
3 ml ($\frac{1}{2}$ level teaspoon)
  baking powder

pinch of salt
75 g (3 oz) porridge oats
125 ml ($\frac{1}{4}$ pint) double
  cream, whipped

Cream the butter and sugar together until they are light and fluffy, then beat in the egg. Mix the baking powder with the salt and porridge oats and stir into the creamed mixture. Using a 5-ml spoon (1 teaspoon), drop the mixture in small amounts on to greased baking trays, spacing them well apart to allow for spreading. Bake at 190°C(375°F)/Gas 5 for about 10 minutes or until the biscuits are firm to the touch. Leave to cool for a few minutes on the baking trays, then remove on to a wire rack. When cold sandwich in pairs with the whipped cream, piping it, using a small star pipe, for a special effect.

Makes 9

Apple Turnovers

213-g (7½-oz) packet frozen puff pastry, thawed
90 ml (6 level tablespoons) apple purée (see page 109)
25 g (1 oz) sultanas
5 ml (1 level teaspoon) ground cinnamon
50 g (2 oz) icing sugar, sifted

Roll the pastry on a lightly-floured board until it is very thin. Trim off the edges and cut out 6 squares. Mix the apple purée with the sultanas and cinnamon and divide between the squares. Moisten the edges of the pastry with a little water and fold over the filling to make triangles. Press the edges gently to seal. Arrange them on a baking tray and bake them at 220°C(425°F)/Gas 7 for 20–25 minutes or until well risen and golden brown.

While the turnovers cook, mix the icing sugar with a little cold water to make a thick icing. As soon as the turnovers come out of the oven, coat them with the icing and serve hot or cold.

Makes 6

Toadstools

1 small egg white
50 g (2 oz) caster sugar
50 g (2 oz) bought almond
    paste
15 g (½ oz) butter, softened

25 g (1 oz) icing sugar,
    sifted
5 ml (1 level teaspoon)
    cocoa powder, sifted
drop of hot water

Whisk the egg white until it is stiff and standing in peaks, then whisk in the caster sugar. Put the meringue into a piping bag fitted with a 1.25-cm (½-in) plain pipe and pipe 20 small rounds on to non-stick paper on a baking tray. Bake the meringues at 120°C(250°F)/Gas ½ for about 1½ hours until they are crisp but still pale.

Soften the almond paste between your fingers, then form it into 20 small stalks.

Cream the butter and icing sugar together to make a butter cream icing. Dissolve the cocoa powder in a few drops of hot water and when it has cooled, beat it into the butter icing to make it chocolate-coloured. Spoon it into a small piping bag fitted with a plain writing pipe and pipe radial lines on the underside of each meringue to look like the gills of a mushroom. Put a blob in the middle of each one and stick the almond stalks in place. Use any icing up by piping spots on the top of the meringues.

Makes 20

Viennese Tarts

225 g (8 oz) butter
50 g (2 oz) icing sugar,
    sifted
175 g (6 oz) plain flour

50 g (2 oz) cornflour
few drops vanilla essence
15 ml (1 level tablespoon)
    red jam

Cream the butter and icing sugar until they are light and fluffy. Sift the flour and cornflour together and fold them into the creamed mixture, adding a few drops of vanilla essence for flavouring. Spoon the mixture into a piping bag fitted with a 1.25-cm ($\frac{1}{2}$-in) star pipe and pipe the mixture into paper cake cases, standing in deep tartlet tins. Pipe into the bottom of each case, then up the sides, working in a spiral movement and leaving a slight hollow in the centre of each one. Bake at 180°C(350°F)/Gas 4 for 20–25 minutes until they are just golden. Cool on a wire rack. If you like, sift a very little icing sugar over the top of each one. Fill the centres with a very little jam.

Makes 12

Cream Horns

213-g (7$\frac{1}{2}$-oz) packet frozen puff pastry, thawed
1 egg white, beaten
25 g (1 oz) caster sugar

60 ml (4 level tablespoons) raspberry jam
142-g (5-oz) carton double cream, whipped

Roll the pastry on a lightly-floured board until it is very thin, keeping it to a good rectangular shape. Trim off the edges and cut it into twelve 2.5-cm (1-in) strips. Lightly grease 12 cream horn tins. Moisten one long edge of each pastry strip and wind it round a cream horn tin, starting from the point. Make sure the moistened edge is facing the tin and that it always overlaps the pastry beneath. Arrange each tin on a baking tray with the pastry end underneath. Bake at 230°C(450°F)/Gas 8 for 10 minutes until golden. Brush the horns with the egg white when you remove them from the oven, sprinkle them with the caster sugar and put them to cool on a wire rack. When cold, gently remove the tins. Spoon a little jam into each horn followed by a little cream. If you prefer, you can pipe the cream into the horns, but you will need a little extra for this.

Makes 12

Frangipane Tartlets

213-g (7½-oz) packet frozen   ½ standard egg, beaten
  puff pastry, thawed   1 egg white, lightly whisked
25 g (1 oz) butter   25 g (1 oz) shredded
25 g (1 oz) caster sugar   almonds
25 g (1 oz) ground almonds

Roll the pastry thinly on a lightly-floured board and cut it
into rounds using a 7.5-cm (3-in) fluted cutter. Cream the
butter and caster sugar until they are light and fluffy. Beat in
the ground almonds and the egg. Put a small amount of the
filling in the centre of half the pastry rounds. Moisten the
pastry edges with water and cover with the remaining rounds,
pressing the edges gently to seal them. Arrange them on wet
baking trays and leave them in the fridge for 30 minutes
to rest. Brush them with the egg white, sprinkle them with
the shredded almonds, and bake them at 220°C(425°F)/Gas 7
for 15–20 minutes until well risen and golden brown. These
cakes may also be finished with a light dusting of icing sugar,
sifted over after they have cooled.

Makes 10

Choux Buns

50 g (2 oz) plain flour   142-g (5-oz) carton double
pinch of salt   cream, whipped
25 g (1 oz) butter   50 g (2 oz) icing sugar
1 large egg, beaten   5 ml (1 level teaspoon)
                                   cocoa powder

Sift the flour on to a piece of paper. Put the salt, butter and
60 ml (4 tablespoons) cold water into a pan. Bring to the boil
and add the flour all at once, removing the pan from the
heat at the same time. Beat well until the mixture becomes
glossy and leaves the sides of the pan to gather in a ball
round the wooden spoon. Allow to cool until you can stand

the pan on the palm of your hand, then gradually beat in the egg. Spoon the mixture into a piping bag fitted with a 1.25-cm ($\frac{1}{2}$-in) plain pipe and pipe 8 mounds on to wet baking trays, making them about 2.5 cm (1 in) high and 7.5 cm (3 in) apart. Cover the buns with deep cake tins and put them in the oven at 190°C(375°F)/Gas 5 for 40 minutes or until the buns are golden brown. Don't uncover them during the cooking because you'll lose all the steam which is making them light. Check only after 35 minutes, sliding a knife under the tin, lifting it quickly up and down again. When they are cooked, allow to cool, then split the cold buns and scoop out any uncooked mixture with a teaspoon. Spoon or pipe the cream into the buns. Sift the icing sugar with the cocoa and mix it to a thick smooth icing with a little cold water. Spoon over each bun and leave to set.

Makes 8

Almond Fingers

100 g (4 oz) plain flour	2 egg whites, stiffly whisked
pinch of salt	100 g (4 oz) ground almonds
50 g (2 oz) butter	100 g (4 oz) caster sugar
1 egg yolk	almond essence
45 ml (3 level tablespoons) raspberry jam	50 g (2 oz) flaked almonds

Sift the flour and salt into a bowl. Rub in the butter and mix to a stiff dough with the egg yolk and about 15 ml (1 tablespoon) cold water. Roll the pastry on a lightly-floured board until it is the same size as a large Swiss roll tin. Grease the tin, then lay the pastry in the bottom. Spread the jam almost to the edges. Whisk the egg whites, then stir in the almonds and sugar and a few drops of almond essence. Spread this mixture gently over the jam right to the edges of the tin, and sprinkle with the flaked almonds. Bake at 180°C(350°F)/Gas 4 for about 35 minutes, or until the topping is golden and springy to touch. Allow to cool in the tin, then cut it first lengthwise down the middle, then across to make fingers. Remove the fingers from the tin with a palette knife. If you have difficulty in removing the first one and it breaks, eat it. That's cooks' perks.

Makes 12

Palmiers

369-g (13-oz) packet frozen puff pastry, thawed

100 g (4 oz) caster sugar
142-g (5-oz) carton double cream, whipped

Roll the pastry on a lightly-sugared board to a 40-cm (16-in) square. Trim the edges to give a good square and to make sure the pastry rises evenly. Sprinkle the pastry generously with some caster sugar and fold in two sides to meet in the middle. Press lightly with the rolling pin and sprinkle with sugar again. Repeat the folding of the sides to the centre, sprinkle with sugar and fold one side on top of the other. Press again with the rolling pin. Dredge with caster sugar. Cut the pastry into 1.25-cm ($\frac{1}{2}$-in) slices and place them on wet baking trays, cut sides down, re-shaping them if necessary. Allow plenty of space between each one for spreading. Bake them at 220°C(425°F)/Gas 7 for 10 minutes or until they are golden, then turn them and cook them until the other side is golden too. Cool on wire racks. Sandwich the palmiers in pairs with the cream, either spreading or piping it on the biscuits.

Makes 10

Mille Feuilles

213-g (7½-oz) packet frozen
  puff pastry, thawed
175 g (6 oz) icing sugar,
  sifted
5 ml (1 level teaspoon)
  cocoa powder, sifted

142-g (5-oz) carton double
  cream, whipped
raspberry jam

Roll the pastry on a lightly-floured board to a rectangle of
0.5-cm (¼-in) thickness. Trim off the edges. Lift the pastry
on to a wet baking tray and cut it into 16 strips, each 10 cm
(4 in) long and 3.75 cm (1½ in) wide. Bake them at 230°C
(450°F)/Gas 8 for about 10 minutes. Cool on a wire rack.

Mix 125 g (5 oz) of the icing sugar to a coating consistency with a little water. Mix the remaining sugar with the
cocoa and a very little hot water to make a piping consistency – thicker than the white icing. Spoon it into a small
piping bag fitted with a plain writing pipe. Spread 8 slices
of pastry with jam and the other 8 with cream and sandwich
together, cream on top of the jam. Ice the tops with the
white icing. Pipe two lines along the top of each cake with
the chocolate icing, then feather this icing by drawing a
knife through it at 1.25-cm (1-in) intervals, first in one
direction then in the other. Work quickly before the icing
sets.

Serves 8

Almond Tuiles

2 egg whites, stiffly whisked
100 g (4 oz) caster sugar
50 g (2 oz) plain flour
3 ml (½ teaspoon) vanilla
  essence

50 g (2 oz) flaked almonds
50 g (2 oz) butter, melted

Whisk the egg whites, then whisk in the sugar. Fold in the

flour, vanilla essence, flaked almonds and melted, but cooled, butter. For each tuile, put 5 ml (1 teaspoon) of the mixture on to greased hot baking trays, allowing a lot of space between each one. Spread the mixture thinly with a fork; if you make a hole it doesn't matter, because they're meant to be lacy. Bake at 190°C(375°F)/Gas 5 for 5–8 minutes until they are a delicate golden colour. Lift each biscuit carefully from the tray and lay it over a rolling pin so that it curls in characteristic fashion.

Makes 25

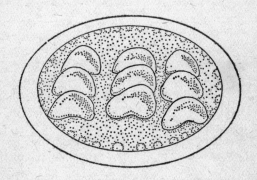

Eccles Cakes

175 g (5 oz) currants
50 g (2 oz) Demerara sugar
2 ml ($\frac{1}{4}$ level teaspoon)
   ground cinnamon
pinch of ground nutmeg
5 ml (1 teaspoon) lemon
   juice, strained

25 g (1 oz) butter, melted
213-g (7$\frac{1}{2}$-oz) packet puff
   pastry, thawed
15 g ($\frac{1}{2}$ oz) caster sugar

Mix the currants, Demerara sugar, cinnamon, nutmeg and lemon juice into the melted butter. Roll the pastry very thinly on a lightly-floured board and cut out 12 circles using a 10-cm (4-in) plain cutter. Divide the filling between the pastry and moisten the pastry edges with water. Gather the edges in the centre and pinch them to seal. Turn the cakes over and roll them more thinly until the fruit just shows through. Make 3 cuts in the top of each one with a sharp knife and place the cakes on a lightly-greased baking tray. Bake at 220°C(425°F)/Gas 7 for 20–25 minutes until the pastry is just coloured. Remove on to wire racks, sprinkle with caster sugar while still hot and leave to cool.

Makes 12

Maids of Honour

213-g (7½-oz) packet frozen puff pastry, thawed
125 ml (¼ pint) milk
30 ml (2 level tablespoons) fresh white breadcrumbs
50 g (2 oz) butter
15 g (½ oz) caster sugar
25 g (1 oz) ground almonds
rind of 1 small lemon, grated
1 large egg, beaten
few drops almond essence

Roll the pastry on a lightly-floured board until it is very thin, then cut out rounds using a 7.5-cm (3-in) fluted cutter. Press the rounds into patty tins. Leave to rest while you prepare the filling.

Heat the milk almost to boiling point, then pour it on to the breadcrumbs. Leave to stand for 10 minutes, then cut the butter into small pieces and beat it in with the sugar, almonds, lemon rind, egg and almond essence to taste. Divide the almond mixture between the pastry rounds and bake them at 220°C(425°F)/Gas 7 for about 20 minutes or until the pastry is golden and the filling puffed up. Cool on a wire rack.

Makes 15

Chocolate Boxes

50 g (2 oz) butter
50 g (2 oz) caster sugar
1 large egg, beaten
40 g (1½ oz) self-raising
flour
15 g (½ oz) cocoa powder
milk to mix
175 g (6 oz) plain chocolate,
melted

Butter icing:
25 g (1 oz) butter
50 g (2 oz) icing sugar,
sifted

30 ml (2 level tablespoons)
raspberry jam, heated

Cream the butter and caster sugar together, then beat in the egg. Sift in the flour and cocoa powder, fold it in lightly and mix to a soft dropping consistency with a little milk. Turn the mixture into a 15-cm (6-in) square cake tin, greased and lined with greaseproof paper. Grease the paper as well. Bake at 190°C(375°F)/Gas 5 for 15–20 minutes or until well risen and firm to the touch. Turn out and cool on a wire rack.

Using the baking tin, mark out on a large sheet of greaseproof paper a shape consisting of 5 outlines touching each other. Spread the melted chocolate all over this shape, right to the edges, trying to make them square. As soon as it begins to set, mark it into 3.75-cm (1½-in) squares and leave it to set.

Cream the butter with the icing sugar for the icing and when it is smooth, spoon it into a piping bag fitted with a small star pipe.

Carefully lift the chocolate squares from the greaseproof paper. Cut the sponge cake into 3.75-cm (1½-in) squares and spread jam around the sides. Stick a chocolate square to each side to form a box. Pipe butter cream along the top of each one, then push the remaining squares into the butter cream to form the lid of the box.

Makes 16

Preserves

This is probably the major preserving season with the pickles and chutneys to be made as well as the everyday jams using fruits such as plums which are fairly cheap, have enough of their own pectin to set well and are a bulky fruit so that you get a lot for your money. Even though you might have done well with tomatoes, when it comes to the very end of the season and you're stripping the plants and pulling them out of the ground, you're still left with a lot of green ones. Besides chutney, you can make jam with both green and red tomatoes so use whichever is most plentiful. And even the tiniest pea-sized examples can go into chutney. I never seem to have the time to make chutney while I'm making my jams and jellies so I bag all my tomatoes and freeze them. Freezing, as you know, breaks down the watery fruits like tomatoes (and strawberries) but this is a process we try and achieve by the long, slow cooking of chutneys, so in the end I'm saving time. You may well get very confused at the different instructions for bottling and covering the various kinds of preserves. Like most instructions in cookery they're based on sound good sense. But the easiest way is to go through the stages step by step.

Jams and jellies go into warmed jars to prevent the glass cracking when the hot preserve comes in contact with it. Because the sugar in the jam or jelly acts as the preservative, you only need a simple covering – a piece of waxed paper pressed close to the surface of the jam or jelly and a cellophane cover stretched over the jar and held by an elastic band, all of which come in packets of jam pot covers found in most stationers.

Chutneys, which are preserved by a mixture of vinegar, spices and sugar, also need to go into warmed jars but because vinegar evaporates, the covering should be as airtight as possible to slow down this process. There's no reason why you shouldn't use jam pot covers as described above if you're going to eat all your chutney in a couple of months. After that, you'll find the top bit of the chutney drying out, turning darker in colour and shrinking. As time goes by, less of the chutney looks moist and more of it looks dried and wizened. A simple but effective way of stopping this is to cover the jars with a piece of linen (an old but boiled hanky will do) and to coat it with melted white candle wax, brushing right over the string fastening. Today you can buy Porosan skin which provides this kind of air-tight covering as effectively, less messily, but at slightly more cost. Pickles, again because of their vinegar, require the same kind of air-tight covering.

When preserving fruits as syrups, the mixture requires sterilisation; the principle being the same as for bottling fruits. Screw-capped, small bottles are best and when these have been filled to within 3.5 cm ($1\frac{1}{2}$ in) of the top, the screw-caps (having been kept under boiling water for at least 15 minutes prior to their use) should be tightened then turned back just a little – not enough to loosen them but just enough to take off the pressure. Processing is a simple affair. Put

the bottles in a pan which will hold them upright plus water
up to the necks of the bottles. Wadded newspaper under the
bottles will prevent the glass touching the metal of the pan,
but will add to the height of the contents. Wadded newspaper
should also be placed between the bottles and the sides of the
pan to prevent glass touching glass or metal. If you have a
thermometer, raise the temperature of the water steadily and
slowly to 77°C(170°F) and maintain it there for 30 minutes.
If you don't have a thermometer, bring the water slowly to
simmering point, when the water moves about, and maintain
as before for 30 minutes. Remove the bottles with oven
gloves, completely tighten the screw-caps and let them cool
on a wooden board. Once opened, keep your syrups in the
fridge, they'll last about 2 weeks, hence the advice to choose
small bottles.

As well as the usual fruits and vegetables found in the
greengrocers at this time of the year, much of the fruits
which are found in the hedgerows, blackberries, sloes and
rosehips, and elderberries in late summer, can be used in
various ways and bearing in mind that the season of giving
isn't far away, I've included some preserving recipes which
make very special presents.

Plum Jam

2.75 kg (6 lb) plums
2.75 kg (6 lb) preserving
   sugar

Wash the fruit and remove any stalks. Cut each plum in half
and remove the stone. Put the plums in a large pan with 750
ml (1½ pints) cold water. If you like, crack some of the stones,
about 40, and remove the kernels. Add to the pan and simmer gently for 30 minutes or until the fruit is soft. Add the
sugar and stir it over a gentle heat until all the sugar has
dissolved, then bring to the boil and boil hard to setting
point.

Test for a set by putting a little jam on a cold saucer and leave it in the fridge for a few minutes. When ready it will wrinkle if you push your finger through the jam. Remove the pan from the heat while you test because it could boil beyond the setting point. This isn't so serious with a large amount of jam; you'll simply have less of it and it may well be a darker colour. But with a small amount of jam, where only 1 kg (2 lb) of fruit has been used, you could find it burns while you test it unless you remove it from the heat.

Allow the jam to stand for 15 minutes or until a thin skin has formed on the surface, then stir it once or twice before pouring it into clean, hot jars and covering the surface of the jam with a waxed disc and the jars with cellophane circles. Stirring it when the jam has cooled a little will prevent the kernels from rising in the jar and should be done for any jam with nuts in it, or whole fruit jam such as strawberry. Label the jam and store it in a cool, dry place.

Makes 4.5 kg (10 lb)

Green or Red Tomato Jam

2.75 kg (6 lb) green or red tomatoes

125 ml (¼ pint) lemon juice, strained

10 ml (2 level teaspoons) citric acid powder

2.75 kg (6 lb) preserving sugar

Pour boiling water over the tomatoes and when the skins begin to split, drain the tomatoes and peel off the skins. Cut them into quarters, or eighths if large, and put them in a preserving pan. Pour in the lemon juice (be generous rather than skimpy with the measure) and add the citric acid powder. Bring slowly to the boil, then simmer the mixture until it is very soft and pulpy. Add the sugar and heat slowly until it has dissolved, then bring to a rapid boil and boil fast until setting point has been reached. Test for a set as described in Plum Jam (see page 164), then pour into clean, hot jars and cover and label.

Makes 2.75 kg (6 lb)

Apple and Blackberry Jam

2 kg (4 lb) cooking apples,   3 kg (6 lb) preserving
  sliced   sugar
2 kg (4 lb) blackberries

Put the apples in a pan with 150 ml ($\frac{1}{4}$ pint) cold water and cook them gently until they are soft. Pick over the black-berries, put them in a pan with 150 ml ($\frac{1}{4}$ pint) cold water and simmer them until they are soft. Combine the fruits in a preserving pan and add the sugar. Heat gently to dissolve the sugar, then bring to the boil and boil until setting point is reached, testing for a set as described in Plum Jam (see page 164). Pour into hot jars, cover and label and store in a cool dry place.

Makes 4.5 kg (10 lb)

Greengage Jam

1.5 kg (3 lb) greengages,   1.5 kg (3 lb) preserving
  stoned   sugar

Put the greengage halves into a preserving pan with 250 ml ($\frac{1}{2}$ pint) cold water. Crack some of the greengage stones – about 12 of them – and add the kernels to the pan. Simmer the fruit for about 20 minutes until it is soft, then stir in the sugar and continue to heat gently until it has dissolved. Bring to the boil and boil hard for about 15 minutes or until setting point is reached. Test for a set as described in Plum Jam (see page 164), then leave the jam to stand for about 15 minutes or until a thin skin has formed on the surface. Stir once or twice, then pour into hot clean jars. Cover and label.

Makes 2.5 kg (5 lb)

Elderberry and Apple Jelly

1.5 kg (3 lb) tart cooking apples
2 kg (4 lb) elderberries
preserving sugar

pared rind of 1 large orange
5-cm (2-in) piece cinnamon stick

Windfall apples are particularly good for jellies if you cut out any damaged parts. They don't have to be peeled and cored, because the peel and cores help the jelly to set, but do rinse the fruit. Put the chopped, prepared apples in a preserving pan. Weigh the elderberries after you have removed the stalks. Put them in the pan with 1 litre (1¾ pints) cold water and bring the fruit slowly to the boil, then simmer them until the apples are really pulpy. Pour the mixture into a jelly bag or into several layers of muslin tied to the legs of an upturned stool and allow the juice to drip undisturbed into a bowl overnight, but cover it with a cloth to keep out dust and fluff.

Next day, measure the juice back into the rinsed pan and add 500 g (1 lb) sugar to every 600 ml (1 pint) juice. Heat gently until the sugar has dissolved, then tie the pieces of orange rind and cinnamon stick together with fine string and add them to the pan. Bring to a rapid boil and boil fast until setting point has been reached, testing for a set as described for Plum Jam (see page 164). Remove the peel and cinnamon. Pour into clean, hot jars, cover and label.

Makes 3.5-4 kg (8-9 lb)

Damson Cheese

1.5 kg (3 lb) damsons
preserving sugar

Rinse the damsons, remove any stalks and put them in a
preserving pan with enough water to come halfway up the
fruit. Bring to the boil and simmer gently for 1 hour or
until the fruit is pulpy and the skins soft. Push the damsons
through a sieve, weigh the purée and return it to the pan
with the same weight of sugar. Heat gently until the sugar
has dissolved. Meanwhile crack the stones and remove the
kernels. Chop these fairly finely and add to the purée. Bring
to the boil and simmer for 1-1¼ hours, stirring frequently
and scraping the bottom of the pan every so often to prevent sticking and burning, as the mixture will become very
thick. Wipe round 1 or 2 straight-sided jars (this preserve
should be turned out of the jar and cut for serving) with a
little light oil and pour in the cheese. Cover well and label,
and keep for at least 6 months before serving. Damson
cheese may be served whole as a dessert, cut into slices at the
time of eating and covered with thick cream, or sliced and
served with cold game.

Makes 1.8 kg (4 lb)

Apple Butter

1 litre (1¾ pints) sweet cider
1.5 kg (3 lb) apples
375 g (¾ lb) Demerara
   sugar
5 ml (1 level teaspoon)
   ground cinnamon
5 ml (1 level teaspoon)
   ground allspice
3 ml (½ level teaspoon)
   ground cloves

Boil the cider in a pan until it is reduced by half, then peel,
core and roughly chop the apples straight into the pan. Cook

the fruit slowly until it is tender, stirring the mixture frequently to make sure it doesn't burn on the bottom of the pan. Push the mixture through a sieve to make a purée and return it to the rinsed pan. Add the sugar and spices, stir well and heat slowly until the sugar has dissolved, then simmer until the mixture thickens. Pour into hot clean jars, cover and label.

Makes 675–900 g (1½–2 lb)

Pear Marmalade

1.5 kg (3 lb) pears
1 kg (2 lb) preserving sugar

juice of 1 large lemon, strained
85 ml (3 fl oz) Certo

Peel, halve and core the pears and keep the peel and cores. Put the pears in a large pan, just cover them with cold water and cook them gently until they are very tender. Remove the pears from the pan with a draining spoon and put the peelings and cores into the pan. Bring to the boil and boil hard until the liquid is reduced by half. Strain it and return it to the rinsed pan. Add the sugar, heat it gently until it has dissolved, then add the lemon juice and Certo and boil it hard until the juice will set, testing for a set as described in Plum Jam (see page 164). Add the pears to the pan and bring them to the boil, then stir them round for 5 minutes until the marmalade is smooth and thick. Cool slightly, then stir to distribute the fruit. Pour into clean, hot jars, cover and label.

Makes 1.5 kg (3 lb)

Plum Sauce

500 ml (1 pint) vinegar	100 g (4 oz) seedless raisins
25 g (1 oz) mixed whole spices	100 g (4 oz) chopped dates
2 kg (4 lb) plums, stoned	225 g (8 oz) brown sugar
225 g (½ lb) onions, finely chopped	25 g (1 oz) salt

Pour the vinegar into a small pan and add the spices. Choose
a mixture of cloves, peppercorns, mace, allspice, cinnamon
stick, mustard seed and root ginger. Bring to the boil, then
remove from the heat and pour into a bowl. Cover with a
plate and leave for 2 hours to cool. Put the plums into a large
pan with the onions, raisins and dates. Strain in the vinegar
and simmer the mixture for 1 hour or until it is very soft.
Push it through a sieve to make a purée. Return this purée to
the cleaned saucepan, add the sugar and salt and simmer it
very gently for 2 hours or more or until the sauce is the consistency of ketchup. Pour at once into heated jars, using
those which have their own screw-top lids. Simmer the lids
in boiling water for 10 minutes before screwing them on to
the jars, making sure they aren't completely tight. Put the
jars into large saucepans with wadded newspaper on the
base and between the jars so that they don't touch each
other or the sides of the pan. Bring to simmering point
(though with newspaper on the bottom of the pan you may
find the water moves quite vigorously) or 77°C(170°F) if
you have a thermometer. Maintain this temperature for 30
minutes, then remove the jars on to a board and tighten the
tops. Allow to cool, then label and store in a cool place.

Makes 1.35 kg (2¾ lb)

Tomato Ketchup

1.5 kg (3 lb) tomatoes, chopped
1 medium-sized onion, chopped
1 large clove garlic, chopped
125 ml (¼ pint) white vinegar

100 g (4 oz) granulated sugar
5 ml (1 level teaspoon) salt
5 ml (1 level teaspoon) cayenne pepper
pinch of paprika

Put the tomatoes, onion and garlic into a preserving pan and cook them together slowly until the onion is really soft, by which time the tomatoes will be very pulpy. Add all the remaining ingredients and continue to cook until, like a chutney, the mixture is thick and has an even consistency. Push the sauce through a sieve to make it completely smooth. Return to the pan and heat the ketchup again, then pour it while still hot into clean hot jars; old ketchup jars are best, the smaller the better, because this preserve should be used up quickly and kept in the fridge once opened. Sterilise the jars as described for Plum Sauce (see page 170). Unopened, your ketchup may be stored with your other preserves in a cool dark place and will keep well.

Makes 1 kg (2 lb)

Green Tomato Chutney

1.5 kg (3 lb) green tomatoes, thinly sliced
500 g (1 lb) cooking apples, quartered
225 g (8 oz) onions, skinned
225 g (8 oz) sultanas
225 g (8 oz) dark brown sugar

15 g (½ oz) salt
375 ml (¾ pint) malt vinegar
25 g (1 oz) mustard seed
25 g (1 oz) whole allspice
15 g (½ oz) dried root ginger

Put the tomatoes in a large pan. Roughly chop the apples and onions and add them to the pan with the sultanas, sugar, salt and vinegar. Tie the mustard seed, allspice and bruised ginger in a small piece of muslin and add to the pan. Bring slowly to the boil, then reduce the heat and simmer the contents until the ingredients are tender, there is no free liquid and the chutney is reduced to a thick consistency. Remove the bag of spices and pour the chutney into clean, hot jars. Cover with screw-tops if you are using screw-top jars or preserving jars. If you use ordinary jam jars, cover each one with a square of linen brushed with melted candle wax for an air-tight seal.

Makes 2 kg (4 lb)

Apple Chutney

1.5 kg (3 lb) cooking apples, roughly chopped
1.5 kg (3 lb) onions, roughly chopped
500 g (1 lb) sultanas
1 large orange
500 ml (1 pint) malt vinegar
675 g (1½ lb) Demerara sugar

Put the apples, onions and sultanas into a large pan. Finely grate the rind from the orange and squeeze out and strain the juice. Add to the pan with the vinegar and bring to the boil slowly. Cook for 30 minutes, then stir in the sugar and heat it slowly until it has dissolved. Continue cooking gently until the contents are reduced to a thick consistency. Pot and cover as described for Green Tomato Chutney (see above).

Makes 2.75 kg (6 lb)

Plum Chutney

1.5 kg (3 lb) plums, stoned
15 ml (1 level tablespoon)
  ground ginger
5 ml (1 level teaspoon)
  mustard powder
25 g (1 oz) salt

15 g (½ oz) whole allspice
12 black peppercorns
12 whole cloves
250 ml (½ pint) vinegar
450 g (1 lb) brown sugar

Put the plums in a pan with the ginger, mustard and salt.
Tie the allspice, peppercorns and cloves in a small piece of
muslin and add to the pan with the vinegar. Simmer the
mixture, covered, for about 1 hour until soft, then stir in
the sugar and continue to simmer, uncovered this time, for
1½–2 hours or until thick. Pot and cover as for Green Tomato
Chutney (see page 171).

Makes 1.5 kg (3 lb)

Autumn Mixed Pickle

0.5 kg (1 lb) button onions,
  skinned
1 large cauliflower,
  prepared
1 head of celery, prepared
1 large cucumber, peeled

1 kg (2 lb) block salt
1 litre (1¾ pints) malt
  vinegar
50 g (2 oz) mixed pickling
  spice
4–6 chilli peppers

Put the onions in a large bowl. Divide the prepared cauliflower into small florets, trimming off any stalks which are
very long. Cut the celery stalks into 2.5-cm (1-in) pieces and
cut the cucumber into 1.25-cm (½-in) dice. Add the vegetables to the onions and mix them well. Cover them with
block salt, shaving it into a powder with a sharp knife.
Leave them to stand for 48 hours. Meanwhile, put the
vinegar and the mixed pickling spice into a pan and bring

it to the boil. Pour the mixture into a basin, cover it with a plate and leave it to stand for 24 hours.

Drain off all the liquid from the mixed vegetables, allowing them to drain in sieves and colanders for an hour or so, then pack the mixture into jars, higgledy-piggledy for family eating, or in an attractive pattern if you wish to give them as presents. Push 1 chilli pepper into each jar. Strain the vinegar and pour it into the jars to cover the vegetables. Cover with screw-tops, if you are using jars which once held pickles, or with pieces of linen, brushed with melted candle wax after tying.

Makes 1.8 kg (4 lb)

Pickled Onions

1 kg (2 lb) small pickling onions	1 litre (1¾ pints) malt vinegar
200 g (8 oz) block salt	50 g (2 oz) mixed pickling spices

Pick over the onions and put them in a large bowl. Don't skin them at this stage. Dissolve the salt, shaved to a powder with a sharp knife, in 2 litres (3½ pints) water. Bring it to the boil, then leave to cool. Strain it and pour half over the onions and leave them to soak for 12 hours. Next day, drain off the brine. Skin the onions, and pour on the remaining fresh brine and leave them for 36 hours. Then drain the onions thoroughly and pack them into jars. Heat the vinegar with the spices to boiling point; pour it into a basin, put a plate on top and leave until it is cold, then strain it over the onions. Cover with pieces of linen brushed with melted candle wax, label and store in a cool dark place.

Makes 1 kg (2 lb)

Spiced Plums

1 kg (2 lb) plums
0.5 kg (1 lb) Demerara
  sugar

5-cm (2-in) piece cinnamon
  stick
malt vinegar

Choose plums that are slightly under-ripe and prick each one with a needle after rinsing them. This will prevent the skins splitting during the cooking. Arrange them in one layer in an ovenproof dish and sprinkle them with the sugar. Add the cinnamon stick and pour in enough vinegar to cover the fruit. Cover the dish and cook the plums at 120°C (250°F)/Gas ½ for about 30 minutes or until the plums feel soft without breaking up. Allow to stand, still covered, overnight. Strain the fruit, keeping the vinegar and pack the plums into jars. Boil the juice, then reduce the heat and simmer it for 30 minutes, until it is reduced and syrupy. Pour over the fruit, cover the jars with a tea towel and allow to cool, then cover them as already described for vinegar mixtures.

Makes 1 kg (2 lb)

Brandied Greengages

0.5 kg (1 lb) greengages
0.5 kg (1 lb) granulated
  sugar

30 ml (2 tablespoons)
  brandy

Choose fruit that is ripe and remove the stalks and weigh afterwards. Then put the fruit in a pan of cold water. Bring the water to the boil slowly and simmer the fruit for 5 minutes, but remove them from the heat and drain them if the skins begin to split before this time. Allow the greengages to drain thoroughly, then peel them carefully, trying to keep them whole. Put them in a large bowl, sprinkle with the sugar and leave them overnight. Put the fruit and sugar

liquid into a preserving pan the next day and simmer them
for about 5 minutes until the sugar liquid turns syrupy. Carefully remove the greengages from the syrup and pack them
into small jars. Boil the syrup for 30 minutes, stir in the
brandy and pour it over the greengages to cover them.
Allow to cool, then cover and store in a cool dry place.

Makes 0.5 kg (1 lb)

Blackberry Syrup

1.5 kg (3 lb) blackberries   preserving sugar

Pick over the blackberries and weigh them after preparing.
Put them in a double saucepan and keep the water simmering underneath, replenishing it when necessary with more
boiling water. Heat until the juices begin to run, then press
the fruit with the end of a wooden rolling pin until the fruit
is really broken down and all the juices have been released
from the seeds. Finally crush the fruit a few more times, just
to make sure. Pour the contents of the pan through a jelly
bag or through several layers of muslin tied to the legs of
an upturned stool and let the juice drip through undisturbed
overnight. Cover the mixture with a tea towel to keep it free
from dust. When all the juice is through, press the pulp
firmly with a rolling pin to extract the last drops of juice.
Pour the juice into a preserving pan, measuring it as you do
so and add 350 g (12 oz) of sugar to each 600 ml (1 pint) of
juice. Stir without heating until the sugar has dissolved, then
strain again through a fine nylon sieve. Pour into clean
screw-top bottles (those which have held bought fruit
syrups or milk shake syrups are ideal) leaving about 2.5 cm
(1 in) headspace. Screw on the caps lightly and stand the
bottles on wadded newspaper in a pan deep enough to hold
water up to the necks of the bottles. Wad more newspaper
and put it between the bottles and the pan to make sure they
don't touch each other or the metal. Bring the water slowly

to simmering point and maintain this simmer for 30 minutes. If you have a thermometer, it should read 77°C(170°F). Remove the bottles and tighten the screw-tops. When the syrup is cool, dip the caps and a little of the neck of each bottle in melted paraffin wax to ensure an air-tight seal.

Makes 1 litre (1¾ pints)

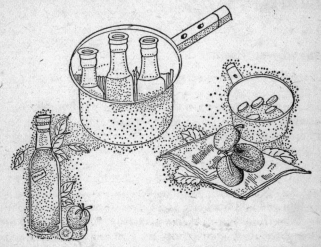

Rosehip Syrup

1 kg (2 lb) ripe rosehips   0.5 kg (1 lb) preserving
                                                         sugar

Bring 1.75 litres (3 pints) cold water to the boil, then wash the rosehips and mince them straight into the pan. Bring back to the boil, remove from the heat and leave to cool, then pour the mixture through a jelly bag or several layers of muslin tied to the legs of an upturned stool. When the juice has drained through, return the pulp to the pan, adding another 1 litre (1¾ pints) boiling water. Repeat the straining

process, then pour the two quantities of clear juice into a
clean pan, bring it to the boil and boil it until it is reduced
by half. Stir in the sugar and heat it gently to dissolve it,
then bring to the boil and boil for 5 minutes. Pour the syrup
into screw-top bottles and sterilise as given for Blackberry
Syrup (see page 176).

Makes about 1 litre (1¾ pints)

Blackberry Brandy

1 litre (1¾ pints) blackberry
   juice (see page 176)
0.5 kg (1 lb) preserving
   sugar
5 ml (1 level teaspoon)
   ground mace

15 ml (1 level tablespoon)
   whole cloves
250 ml (½ pint) brandy

Pour the blackberry juice and sugar into a preserving pan
and heat gently until the sugar has dissolved, then bring to
the boil and add the mace and cloves. If necessary, skim off
the scum from the top at this point. Simmer the mixture for
15 minutes, then remove from the heat and add the brandy.
Pour into a jug, cover the top tightly and leave it for 2 days.
Sterilise some bottles with screw-tops and dry them
thoroughly or drain dry if they are narrow-necked. Strain
the blackberry brandy through several layers of muslin and
pour it into the bottles. Screw on the caps and keep for at
least one month before you sip it.

Makes about 850 ml–1 litre (1½–1¾ pints)

Sloe Gin

sloes   preserving sugar
gin

Use as many or as few sloes as you wish. Rinse the sloes,
remove any stalks and prick each one all over with a darning needle. Put them in bottles, filling them to the shoulders.
Top up with sugar. Slowly pour in the gin to the very top.
Leave for at least 6 months, shaking the bottles every time
you see them – keep them in the kitchen for this purpose.
Sterilise and dry some bottles. Pour the sloe mixture
through several layers of muslin, squeeze the pulp in the
muslin to extract all the liquid, then pour the liquid into the
bottles and seal them. Keep them for at least 6 months before
drinking.

Index

182   INDEX

Biscuits – *contd.*
 Almond Tuiles, 158
 Anzacs, 145
 Cheese Straws, 138
 Chocolate Anytime, 127
 Chocolate Quick Fingers, 128
 Flaky Pinwheels, 127
 Langues de Chat, 150
 Mille Feuilles, 158
 Nutty Potato Cookies, 34
 Oat Thins, 151
 Oatcakes, 24
 Palmiers, 157
 Russian Cigarettes, 149
Blackberry
 and Apple Compôte, 113
 and Apple Dumplings, 126
 Brandy, 178
 Jam, 166
 Syrup, 176
Boxty, 21
Breadbrumbs, Fried, 85
Bubble and Squeak, 20
Butter
 Apple, 168
 Filling, 14
 Icing, 161
Butterscotch Pear Trifle, 126

Cakes
 Apple and Potato, 31
 Apfel Strudel, 112
 Apple Turnovers, 152
 Austrian Curd, 114
 Banana Rum Ring, 143
 Chocolate Boxes, 161
 Chocolate Crackle Flan, 125
 Chocolate Cup, 124
 Chocolate with Potato, 33
 Choux Buns, 155
 Cream Horns, 154
 Devil's Food, 142
 Doughnuts, 34, 146
 Frangipane Tartlets, 155
 Gingerbread, 146
 Greengage Lattice, 144
 Honey Crisps, 128
 Italian Rice, 100
 Jam Tarts, 151
 Little Rice, 101
 Maids of Honour, 160

NOTES